CROP CIRCLES
EVIDENCE OF A COVER-UP

CROP CIRCLES
EVIDENCE OF A COVER-UP

Nicolas Montigiani *1973*

WWW.CARNOTBOOKS.COM

Carnot USA Books
22 West 19th Street, 5th Floor
New York, NY 10011

First edition
Originally published as Crop Circles, Manoeuvres dans le ciel
Translated and adapted by Tom Clegg by Editions Carnot, Chatou, France

Cover design by Priya Kale
Book design by Sharon Lewis
Printed in the United States of America

Library of Congress Cataloguing-in-Publication Data

Montigiani, Nicolas, 1973 -
   [Crop Circles. English]
   Crop Circles: Evidence of a Cover-Up / by Nicolas Montigiani; translated by Thomas Clegg
      p. cm.
Includes bibliographic references.
   ISBN 1-59209-037-0 (pbk. : alk. paper)
1. Crop Circles—Miscellanea.   I. Title.
   AG243.M64 2003
   001.94—dc21   2003010195

Published by:

Carnot USA Books, Inc.
22 West 19th Street, 5th Floor
New York, NY 10011
www.carnotbooks.com

212-255-6505
Email: sales@carnot.fr

To Sophie and Kévin,
with all my love

TABLE OF CONTENTS

Preface

What is a "crop circle?" The word "crop" in English means the harvest or the produce of plants cultivated in a field. By extrapolation, a crop circle is a "circle in the fields." Some people have proposed calling it an "agriglyph," a neologism inspired by "geoglyph," that ageless design conceived and executed since the beginning of time, intended to be seen from the skies above (such as the Nazca designs in Peru). So why not adopt this elegant and fitting appellation?

The authors of crop circles—the heart of the whole mystery surrounding this phenomenon—produce their designs by flattening the cereals growing in the fields. And they draw rather well, the creators of these agricultural enigmas that have caused passionate debate and controversy for over 30 years now.

Over time, crop circles have even come to be considered works of art. These days, they are almost always in wheat fields. Viewed from above (which is necessary since their forms cannot be seen from the ground), they reveal their circles, straight lines, arabesques, symmetries, volutes, or rosettes, in a seemingly never-ending search for greater complexity, greater size, and greater harmony.

Like urban graffiti, they are born in the night. But they are never signed, lacking even the slightest identifying mark, in contrast to the boastful fixation of graffiti artists, who always insist that their spray-painted mural works bear their personal copyright. The agriglyphs we are dealing with here blossom out of nowhere for no apparent reason, defying investigation, making fools of the police, and distressing farmers.

A number of unanswered questions surround agriglyphs:

– Who designed them?
– What techniques were used in their creation?
– Why do they exist?

Regarding their authors, among the prime suspects are "extraterrestrials," for the good reason that the latter would provide a splendid explanation of all three of the enigmas listed above. Extraterrestrials are elusive by nature, since they have supposedly been hiding for centuries in their fast, fleeting, and all-powerful flying saucers. They could very well have created these sudden, vegetal sculptures – thanks to technologies that would necessarily be very advanced. And if they were calling our attention in this way, it would have to mean they were trying to warn us. But about what? That also remains a mystery. Crop circles, according to the supporters of the "extraterrestrial" hypothesis, are marvelous messages that await their "Champollion* of the fields." They are thus the key to the "theses" put forward in almost all the numerous works published on the subject.

*Translator's note: Jean-François Champollion (1790-1832) was the French Egyptologist who first deciphered Egyptian hieroglyphs with the help of the Rosetta Stone.

A second explanation concerns talented pranksters, all too human in origin and fans of creating hoaxes. Alas, neither of these two "explanations" stands up to a close analysis of the facts, as this book will demonstrate.

There exists a third hypothesis which, in our view, is the only one to reconcile fact and logic. It is rational and well-founded, firmly supported by solid scientific arguments. But it will nevertheless prove to be stupefying.

You are invited to join this original "field" study, a journey into the heart of an enigma whose solution is troubling but about which every citizen of the world should be made aware. At long last.

Crop Circles

Chapter One

In A Field Under the Moonlight

The first printed document that evokes some sort of phenomenon dates back to August 22, 1678. It is in the form of an engraving from an old almanac that mentions a "Mowing-Devil." According to this document, the earliest "harvest circle" may have been born out of a quarrel between an English farmer and a mower. It reads as follows:

The Mowing-Devil: Or Strange News Out of Hartfordshire

Being a True Relation of a Farmer, who Bargaining with a Poor Mower, about the Cutting down Three Half Acres of Oats,

upon the Mower's asking too much, the Farmer swore that the Devil should Mow, rather than He. And it fell out, that that very Night, the Crop of Oats shew'd as it had been all of a Flame, but next Morning appear'd so neatly Mow'd by the Devil, or some Infernal Spirit, that no Mortal Man was able to do the like.[1]

---

[1] We have used here the version published by Jérôme Beau, creator of a documentary Web site on the study of UFOs, or flying saucers: http://rro.free.fr/CropCircles.html. NB: The Web links cited in this work may have been modified or have disappeared since the time of writing. This information was published in the French magazine, VSD, hors série (October 2002), p. 37.

The Mowing Devil

This very first crop circle panders to popular imagination because the legend involves intervention by the Devil, of whom extraterrestrials would be the ersatz version today. And no doubt the elliptical design of this demonic harvest does vaguely resemble modern crop circles. But the analogy ends there.

Andreas Müller, one of the world's foremost specialists on the crop circle phenomenon, looked up the first scientific paper on the subject (which dates from 1820) in the archives of the highly respected journal *Nature*. It contains a report on the appearance, that very same year, of numerous circles in a field in Surrey, England.

Much later, in 1963, 1965, and 1967, in Australia, there were several reported cases of bizarre phenomena on the ground, which came to be known as "UFO nests." One was on January 19, 1966, in Tully (northern Queensland), when a circle was discovered among the reeds in a marsh. All along a well-defined perimeter, a layer of plants had been ripped out and lay floating in the water, and three big holes were visible in the middle. The clockwise spiral arrangement of broken reeds, which were intertwined with one another, brought to mind the rotary force of "something" that might have taken off from that spot.

The investigators from the Royal Australian Air Force who were sent to the site discovered two other "nests" nearby. There were no footprints in the surrounding area, which seemed to exclude the possibility of a hoax. (A marsh is not, at first sight, the ideal place to stage such a prank anyway!) The official conclusion was that they were the result of "the action of the strong turbulence that accompanies squalls and storms in the region." And this verdict was accepted.

The agriglyphic annals record another case in 1972, near Warminster, England. On August 12, Bryce Bond and Arthur Shuttlewood described "something" moving about a field and flattening ears of wheat. Two years later, a harvester reported a similar phenomenon.

How long, then, have strange entities been playing in our fields and with farmers' nerves? The historians of agriglyphs have only a vague idea. Some of the sources we consulted indicate that the phenomenon began to appear 50 years ago. The International Crop Circles Archives (ICCA) speaks of 350 "precursor" cases reported prior to the 1980s.

Lacking pictures of any of these enigmatic manifestations in the fields before the end of the 1960s, and thus any concrete evidence or means of reliable, objective analysis (the "pioneers" in studying the phenomenon, Pat Delgado and Colin Andrews, mention seven accounts by farmers between 1950 and 1970),[1] this book will only discuss the more recent appearances that have been verified and photographed.

Circles and Satellites

At the end of the 1970s, the first credible examples of agriglyphs to be recorded appeared in southern England. They were concentrated in two regions, forming part of the so-called "sacred geography" due to the megalithic remains that are to be found there. They include those at Avebury, Silbury, and Stonehenge (in the counties of Wiltshire and Hampshire). In addition to these important sacred places, the favored regions for crop circles have many other remarkable sites: entire fields full of "standing stones," groups of tumuli, and the famous "White Horses," immense pictorial representations executed on hillsides whose authors and dates of origin have still not been clearly determined.

During the "gestation" period of the crop circles, if one may use the expression, the patterns recorded were only simple circles, isolated or in groups (a principal circle, often surrounded by one or several "satellites"). Their sizes ranged from about 10 to 65 ft. in diameter.

As a general rule, the "materialization" of these figures

---

[1] In their book, Circular Evidence, *the first to be published on the subject, and to which we will return below. Bloomsbury, 1989, p. 118.*

occurred on dark nights, usually when it was raining or foggy, and almost always during the summer. The ears of wheat, still on their stems, were ripe. Most of the time, the cereal was flattened in a regular manner throughout the entire surface (at 90 degrees to the plants remaining upright) without having been otherwise affected (i.e., broken or uprooted). The center of some circles conserved a patch of plants measuring a few feet in diameter that had not been flattened. The "brushed" effect, which is most impressive when viewed at a certain distance, was obtained by flattening patches of ears of grain oriented in the same direction. These followed the regular shape of the figure.

All these early circles had one strange point in common: the absence of any witnesses to their formation (with the exception, of course, of confirmed hoaxes). No one, apparently, noticed vehicles parked on the edge of their fields. Late night car travelers have never reported having seen, in the beam of their headlights, suspect nocturnal harvesters. Yet, the record of appearances shows that the phenomenon became more and more frequent over time:

In 1978 – in a field near Headbourne Worthy – that summer, Ian Stevens was at the controls of his harvester combine when he saw before him a vast space in the form of a circle where the wheat had been flattened in a spiral

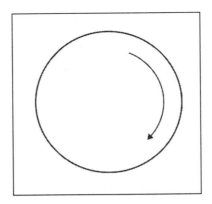

fashion and in a clockwise direction. The farmer decided not to harvest the design immediately so that his wife and daughters could come have a look at it.

In 1980 – near Westbury – in the middle of the month of August, farmer John Scull was annoyed to find that his field of oats had been trampled. At first, he thought it was simply an act of vandalism. But, taking a closer look, he saw that his fields were occupied by three regular circles measuring 65 ft. in diameter! The oats had been flattened and swirled in a clockwise direction. It was learned at this time that the same phenomenon had been witnessed by other farmers who would report having seen other isolated circles in the same region since 1976.

In 1981 – in Hampshire, near Cheesefoot Head – A geometrical figure constituted by a large circle about 55 ft. in diameter, and two smaller satellites about 26 ft. across

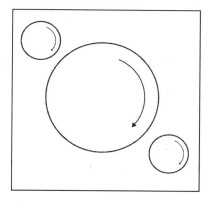

(they were called "triplets") materialized, in a natural circle called the "Punch Bowl." The ears were swirled in a clockwise direction. This design was the first to attract the interest of the general public, since the press, television, and radio reported it. Sightseers flocked to see the figure, beginning a spectacular craze that would continue to grow in the years that followed.

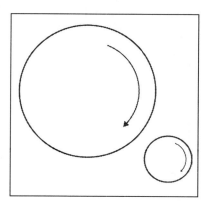

In 1982 – in Litchfield – only a few isolated figures were reported. Two were found in Litchfield (circles of 40 and 30 ft. in diameter) and one in Headbourne Worthy (a circle measuring 38 ft). It is significant that at Litchfield there was also a zone of flattened wheat straddling the field and an adjacent knoll; in fact, it was a semi-circle, since half the knoll was not visible (the grass growing on it was completely unaffected).[1]

In 1983 – The number and complexity of the figures began to increase. The first to mark this overall evolution was a "quintuplet" (a group of five circles) which materialized in a barley field at Cheesefoot Head. It was a circle measuring 52 ft. in diameter surrounded by four smaller ones (13 ft. in diameter) aligned with the cardinal points.

The same year, circular prints also appeared at Westbury (beneath the famous White Horse), near Wantage in

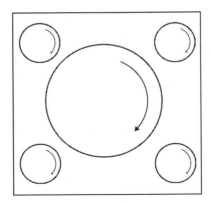

---

[1] *This point is significant. We shall return to it in Chapter Seven.*

Oxfordshire, and not far from Westminster, at Cley Hill. Among the patterns observed there were two superimposed circles of 33 ft., and, for the first time, two parallel bands 265 ft. long and 50 ft. wide, as well as a sort of "ellipse" measuring 13 ft. by 50 ft.

In 1984 – Several quintuplets and a dozen isolated circles were reported, including one at Corhampton in southern Hampshire, a "classic" circle over 80 ft. wide with the ears of grain swirled in a clockwise direction.

In 1985 – The quintuplets were more frequent than ever, still constituted by clockwise circles, varying between 40 and 50 ft. in diameter in the case of the central circles and 10 to 13 ft. for their satellites. The figure found at Matterly Farm was a replica of the one that appeared at Cheesefoot Head in 1983. It took the form of a central circle with a diameter of 50 ft., surrounded by four smaller ones of 11 ft.

Another new development was the sighting of British Army helicopters hovering over the circles.

In 1986 – The circles became still more isolated, and, for the first time, some figures surrounded by a concentric ring appeared. At Cheesefoot Head, ringed circles were discovered on July 5 and August 14. The bigger of the two, measuring 60 ft. in diameter, had a ring that was four ft. wide. The plants in the inner circle were flattened in one

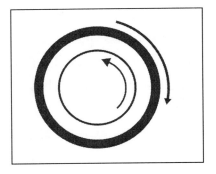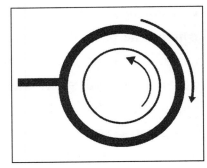

direction, those of the ring in the other!

A circle of about 55 ft. in diameter was observed on August 1, 1986 at Headbourne Worthy. Although it was "classic" in form, it presented one new feature: the ears of wheat were swirled in a counter-clockwise direction. There was another notable evolution that year. At the beginning of September, a circle was found at Childrey with a diameter of 50 ft. (with a 3.5-ft. wide ring swirled in the counter-clockwise direction), to which was attached a seven-foot wide bar.

In 1987 – Double, triple, and quintuple circles were henceforth commonplace (Westbury, Upton Scudamore, Bratton, Winterbourne Stoke). The principal circle of a quintuplet, measuring 65 ft. in diameter (appearing on July 24) presented one peculiarity: the ears were flattened in a radial fashion, from the center outwards, while those of the satellites (10 ft. wide) swirled in a clockwise direction. On August 8, at Bratton, one observed the appearance of a figure with two concentric rings in which the directions of the flattened ears were reversed to one another. Also for the first time, on May 8, 1987, at South Wonston, an isolated circle measuring 47 ft. in diameter was created in a field of rapeseed.

In 1988 – More than 50 agriglyphs (simple circles, circles with rings, triplets, and quintuplets) were found in fields in a period of less than six weeks. There were new developments, such as groups of quintuplets (Silbury Hill, July 25), or the triplet at Corhampton that appeared on June 8, whose ears of grain were "braided" so that a certain relief was given to the formation.

In 1989 – About 90 forms appeared. Located almost exclusively at first in Hampshire and Wiltshire, they had now spread to seven other neighboring counties, as well as Wales, Norfolk, and Scotland. The quintuplets grew bigger

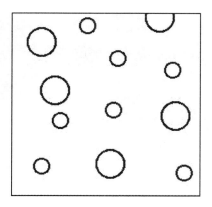

(from 230 to 265 ft. in diameter) and more numerous, while "grapeshot" (multiple circles scattered haphazardly in the same field) made their appearance.

The First Pictograms

In 1990 – A peak in the number of events marked a turning point.

Other than circles with satellites, as at Bishop Cannings, the patterns evolved occurred with new geometric patterns such as "parentheses," half-rings, sinuous forms, bars, and "keys." Certain formations in the shape of dumbbells mixed several different basic forms. "Cereologists" (the name now given to specialists in the study of crop circles – Ceres being the Roman goddess associated with harvests) have taken to calling such complex designs "pictograms."

Often gigantic, these symbols combine circles, rings, various forms of bands, rectangles, and similar shaped objects.

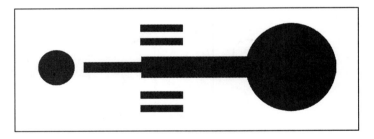

Pictogram that appeared in 1990 at Cheesefoot Head

The giant pictogram at Alton Barnes (413 ft. long) in Wiltshire aroused considerable curiosity after July 12, which led to its worldwide fame. Two thousand people visited the site, and the pattern would even decorate the cover of an album by the rock group Led Zeppelin.

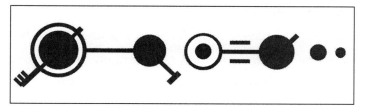

Alton Barnes (analyzed in further detail in Chapter Four)

Starting 48 hours later, this manifestation was followed by 80 new patterns, including triangles on July 25. The farmers, who until then had been hostile to the whole phenomenon as a "crop destroyer," profited from the spectacular popular enthusiasm by exploiting this unexpected form of tourism. They barricaded their fields, and some of them did not hesitate to install caravans at strategic points to collect an entry fee from tourists.[1]

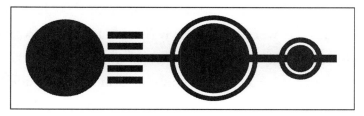

Crawley Downs

---

[1] *This was common practice on the part of "exploiters" of the marvelous. Thirty years ago, Frank Searle, one of the authors of faked photos of the "Loch Ness Monster," camped in a field with his trailer, waiting for visitors. He posted himself there, camera ready. It was clear to an attentive watcher that the spot he had chosen was unsuitable for effective observation. But "donations" nevertheless fell into the tin he left by his trailer-museum.*

It was also during 1990 that the crop circles emigrated from the United Kingdom to the United States, Mexico, South Africa, Australia, Israel, Japan, and throughout Europe. It is impossible to say whether the reports of crop circle appearances across the world are more frequent because the phenomenon is becoming truly widespread, because people have learned to spot and report them, or because we are faced with hoaxes aimed at imitating and discrediting by their numbers the original, exclusively British phenomenon.

In August 1991 – Another "exceptional" year for crop circles. Two Englishmen related a strange experience that happened to them in Surrey, near Hambledon. Gary and Vivienne Tomlinson, walking in the countryside, saw the wheat rippling in a field while a mist rose and a shrill sound was heard. A whirlwind formed, and the hair stood up on Gary's head. The whirlwind vanished, leaving the two witnesses standing dumbfounded in the middle of a circle![1] In the same period, there was the troubling appearance of a message traced in a field at Milk Hill, with strange symbols which, in fact, were later shown (in a study by astronomer Gerald Hawkins) to be a variant of the runic alphabet.

On August 12, a crop circle in the form of a "Mandelbrot set"[2] appeared not far from the University of Cambridge,

---

[1] *Reported in Colin Wilson, Alien Dawn, p. 39. Our bibliographical references are listed at the end of this volume.*
[2] *This was the best known of the fractals whose peculiarity resides in their presentation of an infinite variety of images upon being magnified as much as one desires. Among other Web sites that explain the nature of this phenomenon, see, http://perso.wanadoo.fr/reverrance/graf/fractal/fractal3.htm.*

where Dr. Benoît Mandelbrot, the discoverer of fractals and the related theory concerning nature and chaos, worked. Curiously, the British Army immediately burned the figure.

According to the press, September 8 marked "the end of the crop circle enigma." Two retirees were revealed as the authors of all the figures that had occurred over the last 13 years. In the middle of the night, these "old pranksters," as they would become known, would go into the fields, they said, armed with a wooden board, rope, and other tools to flatten the grain. However, because of certain discrepancies and inconsistencies in their statements, some cereologists soon cast doubt on this testimony, which came "out of the blue" at the height of the crop circle craze. The investigator Andreas Müller would point out that, "Later, the pair were, of course, unable to prove their allegations."[1] The statements of these two men, however, heralded a turning point in the crop circles affair. We will analyze their role in Chapter Four.

In 1992 – Far from dying down, the phenomenon progressed with the appearance of about 180 agriglyphs of ever-increasing complexity.

In 1996 – While previously produced exclusively at night, this year crop circles seemed to be trying to go live, turning up in full daylight, right under the noses of a growing number of observers. Various accounts described a kind of

---

[1] VSD hors série, October 2000, *p. 38.*

fog accompanied by strange sounds that were said to have been measured (at high frequencies of around 5 kHz) while others spoke of "luminous balls" hovering over the fields.

The spiral-shaped "Julia Set," a figure measuring 915 ft. along its curve, constituted by 151 circles, materialized in the space of 15 to 30 minutes, according to witnesses, in full daylight on July 7, in a field near Stonehenge. An analogous agriglyph, but twice as big (over 1,000 ft. across), and with three spiral arms (and hence known as the "Triple Julia Set"), appeared in Wiltshire three weeks later and was the "grand finale" of 1996. Other "creations," including a sort of serpent formed by 89 circles (some saw it as representing a DNA double helix strand) and a gigantic ant, would also mark the crop circle season that year.

In 1997 – Once again, figures with forms of an astonishing quality, including new fractal designs, appeared. The biggest, made on August 8 at Milk Hill, was a giant star composed out of six small curves, inspired by the "Koch Star" and mathematical chaos theory.

In 1999 – One hundred twenty agriglyphs (40 in June, 50 in July, and 29 in August) were found. These included: a sacred chandelier that appeared on May 31; an immense pictogram measuring 1,020 ft. long on June 12 the very first cubical form in three dimensions on June 24; and a star within a circle measuring 330 ft. in diameter on July 16, to which were added more cubical figures in August.

In 2000 – A collection of all kinds of symbols (stars, squares, and even hearts) were found on June 18 at Windmill Hill. One figure in particular stood out. It was a representation of a three-dimensional pyramid contained in a circle. Some would compare it to the "virtual" kinetic art canvas, *Arcturus,* by the painter Vasarely. The next day, in South Field at Alton Priors, a sort of cathedral rosette appeared. On July 19, at Everleigh Ashes, a crop formation was discovered composed of four circles linked by a thin ring, surrounding a sacred, Neolithic round barrow.

Another impressive pictogram came to light at Avebury on July 22: a sort of "magnetic field," whose finesse and complexity aroused wonder.

In 2001 – Older forms (circles) and newer ones (3-D figures) were discovered mixed together. On August 13, on the highest plateau in the county of Wiltshire, at Milk Hill, an impressive pattern of six branches grouping no less than 409 circles (the largest of these measuring 70 ft. in diameter) and covering a surface area of 538,000 sq. ft. appeared. Two days later, an enormous face revealed itself in a wheat field next to the Chilbolton Observatory in Hampshire. The texture of the figure was new, since it consisted in a sort of "crochet" stitching or mosaic, which was very attractive. On August 20, another agriglyph "joined" the face. This was a coded message that some people considered the response to a radio transmission that had been launched towards the stars by the radio telescope at Arecibo, Puerto Rico, back in 1974 and was intended for any eventual extraterrestrial civilizations it encountered. It is reproduced in Chapter Three below and constitutes one of our principal documents for analysis.

In 2002 – Despite the ever-growing number of figures, one fantastic agriglyph, discovered August 15, "eclipsed" all the others. In a rectangle measuring 360 ft. by 250 ft. can be seen a "classic" extraterrestrial face (pear-shaped, with an enormous skull, almond-shaped eyes, and a small mouth), bearing a disc containing a binary code. Cereologists wondered if this message was the key to all the previous messages.

Placebo Effect and Equipment Failures

On the ground, many of those who have visited the crop circles complained of the disagreeable effects experienced in the immediate vicinity of the figures. Symptoms included dizziness, nausea, migraines, or a general sensation of malaise. In addition, there were reports of a buzzing in the ears or strange sounds whose source could not be fixed.[1] Psychologists have evoked the well-known "placebo effect:"

---

[1] *Most of the literature devoted to crop circles mentions testimonies of this nature, including the first such work,* Circular Evidence, *cited in our bibliography, or the more recent study by Eltjo Haselhoff,* The Deepening Complexity of Crop Circles: Scientific Research and Urban Legends, *Frog Ltd. 2001.*

the psyche of a person who expects to feel something when they find themselves at the edge of a place of "exciting" mystery may induce such disorders, exacerbated by apprehension and imagination. But Andreas Müller[1] suggests that, "since a number of the effects reported here have also been observed in living creatures placed in proximity to strong electromagnetic fields, one may be seeing here the action of the energies present at the moment of formation." A possibility that resolute skeptics do not take into account, convinced as they are that only hoaxers could conceive, measure out, and realize, in a few hours, at night, the biggest geometrical figures.

It is much harder to explain the reactions observed in animals (dogs, for example) that refuse to enter the crop formations or betray abnormal symptoms of fright (cries of distress, tails between legs).[2] It is difficult to speak of a "psychological effect" in their case, although some scientists (such as Martin Winckler[3]) assert that animals are perfectly capable of having psychosomatic responses. That cannot explain, however, why electronic equipment (TV cameras, cell phones, etc.) suffers temporary failure or even complete breakdown, as is often reported by those visiting circles.[4]

Very quickly, the fans of UFOs, and among them the most troublesome sort of sectarian gurus, would proclaim their firm belief that crop circles were messages sent from the heavens.

---

[1] *In VSD, hors série No. 5 October 2002, p. 41.*
[2] *Reported by Marie-Thérèse de Brosse, on Europe 1 radio, Sunday, October 13, 2002 at 11 am.*
[3] *On the "Odyssée" radio program, France Inter, January 9, 2003.*
[4] *Several books have recorded reports of this nature. In November 2002, the author of the present work, while standing in the very middle of an old circle, observed that the motor of his Canon EOS 5, a top-quality camera less than a year old, became irremediably jammed. But coincidence, of course, cannot be ruled out.*

Crop Circles

Chapter Two

A Boon to the Cults and UFOlogists

Since its initial manifestations in the late 1970s, the crop circle phenomenon has fascinated people. The "cereologists" who have been trying for over 20 years now to find an explanation have had no success. A host of hypotheses, ranging from the highly rational to the extremely farfetched have been put forward. They have often been ridiculed by scientists and have disappointed the wider public.

Among these are both explanations that point to a "natural origin" for the circles and those that support the notion of "artificial fabrication." The supporters of "bio" solutions to the conundrum attempted to come up with a variety of natural scenarios. Among them are:

- The mycological or "mushroom" hypothesis, which will be familiar to most readers from walks in the country, in meadows, or in parks, where they have seen circular patches of darker grass. It used to be said that these were the marks of the marvelous dances of the fairies, elves, or goblins under the moonlight. The reality is less poetic since these are the result of parasitic infestations of marasmus oreades, also known as "fairy mushrooms." But they cannot explain crop circles since they only develop on grass.

- Another parasitic mushroom, "root rot" (Latin name P. Herpotrichoides), does prefer cereals and for a time was considered to be a prime agriglyphic suspect. However, root rot generally attacks young grain around February. The blighted cereal present brown spots and sometimes fall over, resulting in surprising circular forms. In contrast, the grain flattened within crop circles shows no modification of color. Besides, root rot is not specific to England, and it has never before shown such astounding geometric and mathematical aptitudes.

- How about giant hailstones? The British newspaper, the *Daily Sun,* in an article written by Amanda Cable on July 20, 1990, claimed this was the cause of crop circles, alluding to the fall and subsequent melting of the giant stones in the fields. But alas, even in England, hail would be unable to draw alien heads.

- Psychologically unstable animals have also been nominated. Proponents maintain that crop circles might be produced by deer in rut, the males turning around the females during mating season. Or even better, they blame "mad hedgehogs," turning and turning about under the influence of some version of Saint Vitus's dance.[1]

---

[1] *Suggestion reported by the French magazine,* Science & Vie, *n° 878 (Nov. 1990)*

- Lastly, in 1988, a reader of the *Swindon Times* suggested the collective takeoff of wild geese as an explanation for the circles.

All of these suggestions were almost immediately discredited.

Among the natural hypotheses that have been developed in greater depth is that of an unknown meteorological phenomenon. This idea was defended by the meteorologist and physicist George Terence Meaden, who possesses an impressive *curriculum vitae*.[1] But over time, his view became a big scientific embarrassment.

At the beginning of the 1980s, Meaden joined the still thin ranks of cereologists. Like any self-respecting scientist and in contrast to his then colleagues, Pat Delgado and Colin Andrews, who perceived the work of an intelligent force in the figures drawn in the fields, this meteorologist had no wish to tarnish his reputation. That is why he refused to explain the phenomenon other than through the intervention of "natural forces."

This obstinacy would prove to be his downfall.

After having studied numerous circles, including those that appeared in mid-August, 1980, in a field located near Westbury, in Wiltshire, Meaden soon pinpointed a meteorological cause. But which one?

---

[1] *Holder of a doctorate in physics and Assistant Professor at the University of Grenoble, founder of the Tornado and Storm Research Organization, as well as the Circle Effect Research Group in 1980, he has also been, since 1975, the editor-in-chief of a scientific review,* The Journal of Meteorology.

Could it have been a waterspout? No, because such an event, which is similar to a tornado, forms over a sea or lake (when enormous masses of water are sucked up towards a cloud and fall with devastating impact). Also, a waterspout moves in an uncontrollable fashion and does not extend over 60 ft. wide, especially in Europe.

So might it have been some unknown, never-before witnessed form of a whirlwind? The latter explanation is not much more convincing, although Meaden noticed that the circles tended to appear at the base of hills. A whirling wind sweeping across a height might, under certain circumstances, create a mini-tornado when it met a mass of air immobilized by a hill. The internal friction would charge the mini-tornado with electricity. By moving in centripetal or centrifugal fashion over a field, a mini-tornado could descend upon the grain and form a circle. This could constitute a novel phenomenon, similar to ball lightning, but without its calorific effect. Meaden firmly believes in this theory and has baptized it with the label of "plasma vortex."

But it has been difficult for him to explain the general and progressive evolution of the phenomenon over a period of several years, with more and more complex patterns, often located further away from hills. Furthermore, he has been unable to explain how the satellites of a big circle were smaller and aligned with the cardinal points. Similarly, what about the rings that were found surrounding certain circles? Why, up until 1986, was the grain always swirled in a clockwise direction, whereas, after that date, one began to find counter-clockwise examples? Could a mini-tornado have formed triangles like those found in 1990? All of these are questions that "cold plasma" has trouble explaining. But Meaden is a stubborn man, adapting his arguments according to each year's "consignment" of crop circles. Those that he can't explain, he just classifies among the hoaxes.

If the theory of an electromagnetic vortex "reassured" the scientific community, it was definitively discredited when, in 1990, the first astonishing pictogram appeared at Alton Barnes.

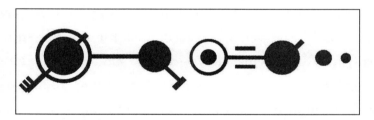

The "Pictogram" of Alton Barnes: Was it the work of a plasma whirlwind?

The 415-ft.-long pattern is made up of several circles, some of which sport outgrowths (in the form of keys) and are linked by "avenues." Thereafter, it was completely clear that a natural cause, however extraordinary, could not produce patterns with such geometrical coherence. Doubtless, Meaden was annoyed by this pictogram. But far from admitting defeat, he declared that he just needed a little more time to explain it. Would the plasma vortex theory have to be adapted to fit the facts? Decidedly, in doing so, George Terence Meaden will have contributed more to discrediting the scientific approach than to serving it.

Nevertheless, luminous balls as large as grapefruits that witnesses claimed to have seen above the fields before the formation of a crop circle did, for a time, revive the "plasma" hypothesis. During the 1960s, the physicist Philip Klass was convinced of the existence of a link between these rare electrical phenomena and claims of UFO sightings. According to Klass, the proximity of high voltage power lines could very well have accounted for the presence of small, furtive, moving glows—a new kind of Saint Elmo's fire—that witnesses saw dancing or flitting about in an erratic fashion in the countryside, confusing them with an extraterrestrial phenomenon.

Unfortunately, this theory could not explain agriglyphs, as the great majority of fields in Wiltshire or Hampshire (which our own on-the-spot investigation confirmed) are not near high voltage lines. The English countryside is extremely well-preserved and practically free of even the smallest unsightly electrical pole. And if electrical causes were responsible for some strange apparitions (and it must not be forgotten that these novel kinds of plasma have never been observed or reproduced in the laboratory), it is of course completely out of the question that they could have such artificial forms.

Another natural cause, that was labeled the theory of "lines of force," took shape when dowsers, with the aid of their wands, noticed that certain crop circles followed ley lines, the network of lines of force that were detected, traced, and channeled in prehistoric times, and whose nature and meaning is unknown to us today. In 1988, circles materialized on the "Mary Line."[1] As a result, some have suggested that "spirits of nature," generative divinities, and other "elementals" are trying to send us a subtle and esoteric message. According to them, the proximity of circles to ancient megalithic prehistoric sites, which some believe emit an enigmatic energy that our ancestors discovered and knew how to use, is thus justified (see the work of Paul Devereux and his "Dragon Project"[2]).

Is all this activity, only hallucinations, hoaxes, or the skeptics' favorite explanation, rare weather or electromagnetic phenomena? No, because none of these stand up to scrutiny. A natural phenomenon (ball lightning, will-o'-the-wisps, Saint Elmo's fire,[3] suspended ice crystals

---

[1] This alleged ley line runs from Mount St. Michaels in Cornwall to the east coast of England near Hopton.
[2] The British researcher, Paul Devereux, is an enthusiast of ancient sites, unexplained phenomena, "psychedelic prehistory," and UFOs. His "Dragon Project" is a study of magnetism, radiation, unexplained luminous phenomena, and other strange manifestations around sacred sites: see The Leyhunters Companion, Thames & Hudson Ltd., 1979.
[3] A manifestation of the "corona effect," when an electrical field in proximity to a conductor is strong enough to provoke a discharge in the surrounding air and excite the air molecules, which then emit a characteristic light.

deforming natural lights, mirages, etc.) at first sight hardly has the capacity to behave in an intelligent and coordinated fashion, especially when the objects are multiple. But then again, to simply reject certain witness accounts on the subjective pretext that they seem "crazy" or impossible" is not at all satisfactory. In reality, these testimonials clearly contain features that are familiar "constants" concerning UFOs, including the recurrent theme of "intelligent behavior."

Similarly, for those who support the "Gaïa hypothesis,"[1] crop circles may constitute a message or a warning addressed by a dying earth to the human species demanding a little respect.

People are free, of course, to believe what they will about all this.

The Andrews and Delgado UFO Thesis

From the very start of the crop circle appearances, pragmatic British farmers suspected nocturnal military activities. Might not the circles be the result of the action of helicopter rotor blades, and in particular, those of the double rotor American Chinook? A British Ministry of Defence (MOD) spokesman raised this hypothesis, quite seriously, in an article that appeared in the *Southern Evening Echo* on August 28, 1981. But it soon became apparent that the downdraft from helicopter rotors can only produce vague

---

[1] *The idea that our planet is a being in its own right, a living super-organism.*

bowl-shaped traces and not marks with sharp, crisp edges like those found in crop circles.

Supporters of the rotor hypothesis, however, have not given up. They suggest (without any sense of irony) that the helicopters may have been flying upside down! For its part, the British army has always denied any involvement in the phenomenon.

One farmer, whose field was the victim of a crop circle, told the *Daily Express* (July 27, 1990) that the patterns were created by laser beams projected on the ground by military planes. Aerostats—dirigibles or balloons—have also been suspected. These types of aircraft, silent by nature, would permit nocturnal over-flights (thus explaining the lack of traces in surrounding areas) and their powerful compression engines could produce the forms found in the fields. These "flying artists" would, however, be taking some very big risks, because night flights are forbidden in England.

One theory formulated at the end of the 1980s, still finds powerful support. It is based on the fact that, in "95 percent of cases, the grain flattened inside crop circles shows no sign of any damage and is neither broken nor crushed."[1] Its authors are Colin Andrews and Pat Delgado.[2]

Andrews and Delgado, who were pioneers in the field of research on crop circles, began their work in 1981. George Terence Meaden joined their team, but soon followed

---

[1] Circular Evidence, *op cit., p. 154.*
[2] *Andrews was an electrical engineer at the research department of Test Valley Borough Council in England, while his partner worked for the British Missile Testing Range and for NASA.*

another line of research. In 1989, Andrews and Delgado published the first work devoted to the phenomenon, *Circular Evidence.*

This book, which appeared at the height of the frenzy provoked by the "circular marks" (and made it a veritable bestseller in Britain, where even Queen Elizabeth is said to have read it) offered a serious, detailed study of 25 crop circles that appeared between 1978 and 1988. The authors developed in this work a novel and impressive idea. In view of unexplained incidents that took place during their investigation, such as a compass that went "crazy," whistling, and low frequency sounds, blue-colored flashes, or technical malfunctions of their electronic equipment, the authors speculated about "unknown powers" that might have caused phenomena of this nature. For them, there was little doubt that a force was at work, but what was it?

In this radically new vision, they expressed the idea that the circles could be interpreted as messages addressed to humans by an intelligent agent, produced by a technology still unknown to us. To support the hypothesis that extraterrestrials could be behind all these events, Andrews and Delgado reported several accounts of UFO sightings linked, it would seem, to the appearance of crop circles. Here are a few of these accounts:

- On the evening of July 6, 1985, as they were driving on the A273 highway in Hampshire county, Pat and Jack Collins said they saw an enormous circular object, like a Ferris wheel, viewed from the side as it hovered near the ground. The following morning, five circles were found in Alresford field at Matterley Farm.
- During the night of July 9, 1987, at Cheesefoot Head, near the place called the "Punch Bowl," Martin and Petronel Payne sighted luminous spheres behind a row of trees. These spheres seemed to "dance" and play "leap frog." The next day, a circle with a ring was discovered nearby.
- On the morning of July 13, 1988, near the ancient megalithic site of Avebury, Mary Freeman saw, among the clouds, a large object in the form of a yellow disc that was sending a beam of light towards a field behind the giant mound of Silbury, not far from the spot where she was standing. The next morning, 10 circles (in fact, two quintuplets, each comprised of a principal circle with four satellites) were counted in that field.

For some people, the link between these strange phenomena and the appearance of patterns in the fields can be quickly made. On July 26, 1990, the *Western Daily Press* had no qualms in writing: "The great density of ley lines is perhaps at the origin of a force field, making Wiltshire an admirable target for a high-definition laser employed at the other end of the galaxy to communicate with us." Some journalists will stop at nothing to provide a good story.

To try to gain a clearer picture, let's look at the strange world of ufology and examine its facts, its excesses, and its digressions.

An Insult to the Prime Minister

It used to be one of the most closely guarded places in the world.

Here, elite British troops patrolled the dozens of acres of grounds round-the-clock, ready to face any type of threat, including terrorist attacks or aerial bombardment. Here being the country residence of the British prime minister of the time, John Major, a sensitive, high-security site.

And yet, a crop circle in the form of a cross appeared in a field within the grounds in July, 1991.[1] The figure was perfectly formed, with something resembling an arrow at the top aimed directly at the prime minister's residence.

What nerve!

It was enough to give nightmares to the men in charge of security because the pattern's mysterious artists were not, it seemed, deterred by the exceptional deployment of guards protecting the property from any intrusion. But the strangest

[1] *See report at* www.lovely.clara.net/crop_circles-history91.html.

detail of all remains the explanation that John Major himself gave to journalists inquiring about the event. In response to the question of whether a security breach had taken place, the PM replied that the figure was merely "the result of poor soil conditions." No doubt this was an example of English humor. But this curious explanation of such an incident led to considerable speculation on the part of the media. On July 11, one newspaper carried the headline: "Now Explain This!"[1]

For the journalist who wrote the article, it was a matter of finding out what manner of individual(s) would be crazy or irresponsible enough to penetrate a private, restricted area under close watch, with the risk of being shot if he (or they) were discovered, and take the time to complete a design whose meaning was far from obvious.

Who could successfully undertake such an astounding project? Who would dare defy the best government agents of Her Majesty with such ease? This strange affair was not going to bring credit to the British government concerning the security of its territory. Terrorists would be delighted.

But while the prime minister spoke of "poor soil conditions" at his private residence, some saw no mystery at all in this incident because it only confirmed what they already knew. Their reasoning was simple. Since it was difficult, almost impossible, to explain such an exploit

---

[1] See www.dailyrevolution.org/allgood/010420.html.

through conventional hypotheses, more extraordinary ones needed to be envisaged. And among these, the "unknown intelligent force" thesis, already seriously evoked since 1989, was best able to account for this superhuman feat, this "challenge" to the highest levels of the British state.

"They" Are Writing to Us

"Someone" is trying to contact human beings and seems able to do so wherever and whenever they like. What else besides a "superior intelligence" would be capable of achieving this? Does one not have here all the ideal and logical components of a first contact scenario between this "intelligence" and mankind? If not, how does one explain the absence of tracks among the plants, the speed of execution, and numerous other surprising aberrations that define the general phenomenon?

All this time we have been waiting for them! One of the most basic questions posed by humanity, "Are we alone in the universe?" has finally been answered.

And what an answer!

"They" are writing to us. "They" are trying to communicate with us, and the manner in which "they" are doing so is as subtle as it is unstoppable, both logical and sensible.

Circles, double circles, "ringed" circles, lines, rectangles, triangles, curves, squares, spirals, esoteric and cabalistic symbols, planetary systems, three-dimensional pyramids, crosses, mathematical formula, and even "their" face, a whole assortment of "pictograms" of growing difficulty, patiently and perfectly evolving over time, all these confirm that "they" are, in fact, out there and are seeking to prepare us, gently, for the idea of a measured, calculated form of exchange.

Mediums, magnetizers, and other "vibration-sensitive" individuals are equally adamant. They all feel in their bones (or through the intermediary of instruments such as dowsing wands or pendulums) a superior, inexplicable "remanent force" residing in the agriglyphs. Haven't visitors felt a curious sense of oppression or malaise in the vicinity of crop circles? And electronic equipment has broken down in an unaccountable fashion. That is indeed proof, ufologists claim, that "someone" is employing a mysterious force in the production of these figures and their message. Crop circles are a highly evolved means of communication.

That, in any case, is what many people believe.

In support of this miraculous explanation, there are several troubling accounts that have cropped up in the past which seem to validate the idea of "external" intervention. The oldest of these coincide with the appearance of figures at the end of the 1970s. Small luminous spheres were regularly seen above or nearby fields where agriglyphs were later found. In addition to these curious, furtive manifestations, some veritable "close encounters" with massive craft that seemed to come straight out of a science fiction tale had also begun to emerge.[1] And these "flying saucers" seemed to be closely involved in the materialization of "field art."

Why the "UFO" Thesis Has Triumphed

Enigmatic and elusive, unidentified flying objects have regularly appeared in the news since 1947, the year Kenneth Arnold sighted unusual disc-shaped craft moving at high speeds (the figure of 1,300 mph was mentioned) in the skies over Washington state. Since then, tens of thousands of sightings have occurred across the world; reports of giant "vessels" in the form of saucers or cigars, or else balls of light, crossing the skies in violation of elementary laws of physics and aerodynamics; stationary hovering; sudden accelerations; etc. Not only have these disturbing apparitions traversed our airspace with great ease, but they have played cat-and-mouse with fighter planes sent to intercept them. When they have manifested themselves within or in proximity to crop circles, their effects on electrical circuits (extinguishing car headlights and radios,

---

[1] See the accounts by Pat and Jack Collins, or by Mary Freeman, briefly cited above.

stalling car engines, and even causing blackouts in homes beneath their flight path) have often been mentioned.

What are UFOs? To some, they are natural phenomena, to others hallucinations. But the public is willing to accept that humanity is dealing with spacecraft or machines from some other dimension, piloted by entities whose nature is still unknown.[1]

For supporters of the theory of gradual contact, these intelligent beings decided, after a long phase of observing our actions and behavior, to "move into higher gear," that is to say, enter into a dialogue with us. But take note that they have done so neither directly nor suddenly, at the risk of seeing terrestrial civilization collapse when faced with a truth it is still not ready to accept, either culturally or scientifically. The dialogue must occur gradually, with all manner of precautions and over a period of decades, which, for those who hold this view, will help to prepare our minds in a gentle fashion.

But how would this be carried out? How would such a form of communication be conceived and what would be its material support? In the 1970s, the great American astronomer, Carl Sagan, described "eventual contact" in the following way: "The message will be founded on elements common to both civilizations, the transmitter and the

---

[1] According to various opinion polls carried out in recent years, fully half of the population in Western countries believes in the existence of intelligent extraterrestrial life. Among them, Americans are the champions in their belief of contacts with "visitors."

receiver. What are these common elements? Certainly not a written or spoken language, nor any element of the instinctual coding inscribed in our genetic material; but rather, that which we share—the universe that surrounds us—science and mathematics."[1]

Mathematics, a source common to our species and "them," is perfectly suited to serve as the basis for dialogue. And agricultural fields would of course be the material support for "engaging in conversation."

In keeping with this kind of scenario, the supporters of the "contact" theory have reconstructed the supposed reasoning of the alleged "intelligences" as follows. Through terrestrial reconnaissance missions, the "visitors" have seen that humans, to nourish themselves, cultivate grain cereals as a staple of their food source, on large tracts of land. The extraterrestrials have technology capable of modifying the molecular state of these plants—bending them from a distance, for example. Crop fields are thus the ideal canvas for sending messages, which are being increased in complexity over time, in order to accustom and convince the population. Small, discreet, and rapid probes are sent to carry out this task because, according to reports, these small, metallic machines, often spherical in form (or simply "balls of light"), that have been sighted around the English fields, are responsible for the materialization of agriglyphs.

[1] The Cosmic Connection: An Extraterrestrial Perspective, *Doubleday, 1973.*

Everything leads to the conclusion that, if we are, in fact, confronted with physical machines, these small "autonomous units" are remote controlled drones dropped by a "mother ship" lying in wait at high altitude, or indeed, out in space.

One of the principal accounts suggesting such a scenario goes back to one of the first officially reported cases, of crop circles. It occurred on September 1, 1974, in Saskatchewan, near the city of Langenburg, in Canada. That morning, farmer Edwin Fuhr was harvesting his wheat field when he saw five metallic-looking "little domes" a few dozen feet away from him in a grassy spot. Fuhr got down from his harvester and approached the objects. He realized with horror that they were floating a few feet above the ground and were disturbing the grass beneath them. Shaken by the experience, the farmer climbed back onto the harvester, from where he saw one of the machines suddenly rise into the air, soon joined by the others. All of them were now 100 ft. in the air, and stationary once again, when jets of vapor escaped from small nozzles at the base of each machine, followed by a strange blast that flattened the wheat in his field. After a few minutes, the objects rose and finally disappeared into the clouds. In the field, several circles of flattened wheat, swirled in a clockwise direction, bore witness that something had occurred.[1]

There is an abundance of similar accounts. In 1997, for

---

[1] *Cited in Colin Wilson,* Alien Dawn, *p. 38.*

example, some vacationing Czechs said they had seen small "luminous balls" moving above a field where a crop circle was found the next day near the White Horse at Alton Barnes.

Thus, very soon, the circles were associated with a technology that surpasses, by a wide margin, that achieved by our science at the beginning of the twenty-first century – including stationary hovering and the flattening of wheat from a distance. Furthermore, the case of the Saskatchewan farmer closely resembles another more recent report, this one from France. On January 8, 1981, at Trans-en-Provence, in the southeastern département of Var, Renato Niccolaï saw a metallic object in the form of a saucer about seven feet in diameter. "Descended from the sky," it landed on a terrace of land several dozen feet away from him. The machine took off a few seconds later, with a slight whistling sound, leaving behind a small cloud of dust.

The world of ufology has thus become excited about crop circles, which fit in well with the "contact" theory. But material evidence (such as video recordings) is cruelly lacking, despite what naive Web surfers may think.

Faked Video Evidence

There is considerable "video evidence" available on the Internet. The first time one views one of these online documents, there appears to be reason for enthusiasm. One gets the impression of having, before one's eyes, the proof of the extraterrestrial origin of crop circles! One can make out – rather badly, in blurry videos – a number of small spinning spheres, while figures appear in the wheat field out of the flattened grain.

However, a quick investigation suffices to discredit these as montages put together by pranksters. The best known and the most impressive of these videos lasts less than 30 seconds. It is supposed to have been filmed on the morning of August 11, 1996, by an unnamed man from the ramparts of Oliver Castle, near Devizes in Wiltshire. The short video[1] begins with a perfectly ordinary wide shot of an even more ordinary field. Suddenly, two small "balls of light" burst into view from the right-hand side of the frame flying about 30 ft. over the ground and circling in a clockwise direction. Underneath the rapidly revolving spheres, certain parts of the plants under cultivation brusquely begin to vibrate and are flattened as if by some mysterious force. As the first two spheres rapidly leave the field of vision, a third one appears, from the left, to finish creating a giant pattern in the shape of a snowflake. It seems incredible but is nonetheless faked.

The expert, Colin Andrews, very quickly exposed this dubious document. How is it that the field was being filmed before the appearance of the flying machines, at precisely the spot (and framed so tightly) where the spheres would

---

[1] *Which can still be viewed at* www.facteurx.fr.st

appear? It's as if the person taking the shot expected that this spot would very soon be visited by a mysterious phenomenon. This circumstance alone renders the film suspect.[1] To settle any doubts, we asked an expert on videos in the crop circle domain, Peter Sorenson. His response was unambiguous: the film was definitely a hoax for the good and simple reason that he'd met the "director," a special effects wizard.[2]

Pictures no longer constitute proof. Increasingly sophisticated software allows the creation of computer-generated images which seem more real than the real thing. The recent film *Red Planet,* starring Val Kilmer, is a good example. The Martian landscapes are depicted with complete realism. It is henceforth futile to imagine that crop circle videos will be immune from attempted fakes.

But there is a greater danger than film hoaxes: that of sectarian abuses.

Raël and Company

Religious sects have not let the opportunity to profit from crop circles slip away. The phenomenon could not have emerged at a better moment to comfort and serve the ends of certain groups among them, including the Raëlians.

What a godsend they have proved for "His Holiness"

[1] *See* www.swirlednews.com/article.asp?artID=509.
[2] *Email dated August 13, 2002.*

Raël, a specialist in media exploitation, as the recent affair with faked human clones has shown. By exploiting the "message" of circles, said to be "signs" from "pacific extraterrestrials" for whom he claims to be the appointed bishop on earth, the extremely wealthy Claude Vorilhon has succeeded in co-opting the "agriglyph effect" at little cost.

Vorilhon claims that, in 1973, while walking (alone, naturally) in the countryside of the Auvergne region in France, he met a visitor from space who had suddenly descended from a luminous flying saucer. This was not just any "E.T.," but the "President of the Council of the Eternals" in person! He proceeded to tell Vorilhon the true story of creation. The extraterrestrials, who call themselves the Elohim and are inhabitants of a planet 5.5 billion miles from Earth, selected our world a very long time ago as an immense cloning laboratory to create mankind and all forms of life. In the course of this meeting, the president from space appointed Vorilhon as a messenger, destined to prepare for the return of our divine creators, now in need of dialogue with their children. The messenger would call himself Raël from that point onwards and was the "Chosen One," who would construct an embassy to welcome them on the fateful day.

The theme is not original. From the "suicide" of 69

members of the Order of the Solar Temple in the early 1990s to that of the 39 members of the Heaven's Gate cult a few years later, one finds the same recipes as those used by the founder of the Church of Scientology, L. Ron Hubbard, who also claimed to be in contact with a council formed by nine extraterrestrial entities.

How did Raël co-opt crop circles? By offering the "keys to the enigma."[1] A certain Marcel Terrusse (a Raëlian "Guide-Bishop") delivered the truth about the pictograms: "Crop Circles have a non-human origin, and from this perspective it has to be understood that we are dealing with an unknown technology in advance of our own."

Under the title, "The Raëlian Religion and Crop Circles," Terrusse returns to the theme of preparations for contact: "The interpretation that we can give them is that they constitute an application of the strategy for preparing official contact between men on Earth and an extraterrestrial civilization."

The problem with this "interpretation" by the "chosen ones" is that it contains nothing new. It's the familiar, well-worn, and over-exploited science fiction cliché that oscillates between belligerent extraterrestrials and messianic aliens anxious to establish progressive contact in a manner that allows the humans to grow accustomed to their peaceful presence.

---

[1] See www.chez.com/cropcircles , but be warned, this site is run by the Raëlian sect.

Peaceful? The E.T.s of the Raëlians appear to endorse the practice of eugenics, which consists in eliminating, at the fetal stage, the physically and mentally handicapped. This explains why Raël wants to be the first to attempt human cloning, which he claimed to have succeeded in doing at the end of December 2002, through Clonaid, the company he largely financed.

All of this is singularly unimaginative. "What is underway, beyond the marks on the ground, is a manifestation of an openly physical nature. At that stage, we really will be entering a new age," concludes "Bishop" Terrusse.

Does the favored location of the agriglyphs—southern England, at the heart of the most ancient megalithic sites—play a role in this "New Age"? "New Age" adepts—like the cults—would have us believe so. But from here onwards, we will line up arguments against this new irrational hypothesis.

Crop Circles

Chapter Three

Exposing the Extraterrestrial "New Age"

The first crop circles to be reported materialized in England at the end of the 1970s in the counties of Wiltshire and Hampshire. And nowhere else.

Is it merely coincidence that these two counties are also home to major archeological sites and richly endowed with standing stones and barrows, among the ancient traces of human endeavor (Avebury Henge, Silbury Hill, Windmill Hill, West Kennet Long Barrow, Stonehenge, Woodhenge, Durrington Walls, Normanton Down, etc.)? Is it a coincidence that the majority of agriglyphs are near these megalithic groups? The "New Age" adepts will reply "no" without the slightest hesitation.

The term "New Age" is quite difficult to interpret. It emerged towards the end of the 1960's as a sort of prolongation of the hippy movement. It promotes simple values and refuges such as peace, ecology, and personal spiritual development. Analysts like Lynn Picknett and Clive Prince have attempted to give very rough estimates of its numerical strength: "No one knows exactly how many individuals belong to this movement, which has attracted followers from California to Glastonbury, and even to the ashrams in India, but there must be hundreds of thousands, if not millions, of people."[1]

Undoubtedly, crop circles have given the movement a second wind, so to speak. We offer as proof a lecture series given by a firm specializing in the field of divination. Its title,"The Mysterious Crop Circles: Language of Our Earth, Expression of the Universe," sums up its "philosophy:" On January 31, 2003, in Paris, the lecturer, a cereologist working in the field, showed several hundred slides of agriglyphs for an entrance fee of €15 ($15), in front of a captivated audience whose "oohs" and "aahs" greeted each new picture with ecstatic bliss. For the "circle fanatic" presenting these figures, they are the magical message of a universe which felt compassion for humanity. Perceiving in them "sacred symbols of the earth's elders: voodoo, Amerindian, Celtic, Egyptian, and cosmic in origin," she explores, photographs, and draws the new designs that emerge each year, upon which she likes to "meditate."

She is far from alone. In the vicinity of the megalithic sites of southern England, she sometimes joins in the new pagan rites which the modern New Age "Celts" have adopted, dancing amidst the wheat in white robes—sometimes braving the gun of an exasperated farmer—and playing the harp.

---

[1] *Lynn Picknett & Clive Prince,* The Stargate Conspiracy: The Truth About Extraterrestrial Life and the Mysteries of Ancient Egypt, *Berkley, 2001.*

The Megalithic Circle of Stonehenge. What connection is there with the neighboring vegetal circles?

And it goes without saying that crop circles are prolific at these sacred sites. The megalithic temple of Stonehenge (derived from the Saxon for "hanging stone") in Wiltshire is undoubtedly the most famous site, mysterious and millennia old, venerated by a growing number of New Age adepts who have also become fans of the agriglyphs (90 percent of crop circles have manifested themselves within a radius of about 45 mi. from Stonehenge).

Stonehenge today remains a mystery. The enormous, unique monument stands on the windy Salisbury plain, a chalk region about 80 mi. west of London. It is the only megalithic circle whose stones were carefully shaped by man. A vast ditch, measuring over 300 ft. in diameter, surrounds the principal complex. This was originally a continuous circular portal formed by 30 standing stones composed of sandstone, each of them 16 ft. high and weighing about 25 tons. They are surmounted horizontally by 30 enormous lintels which follow the curve of a circle. The biggest weighs 40 tons and measures 30 ft. long. They come from Marlborough Downs, 18 mi. away.

Inside this is another circle constituted by nearly 80 stones, 6.5 ft. tall and weighing four tons each. Experts have determined that they originated in the quarries of Preseli Hills in southwestern Wales, 150 mi. away.

The association of this site with extraterrestrials, the new era, and crop circles was inevitable. For the New Age adepts, "The circles and pictograms in the cultivated fields are the phenomenological expressions of consciousness. They appear in your reality to show you that the rational spirit cannot control all information as it would like to do. [...] The circles and pictograms completely surpass the logical spirit's interpretative capacity."[1] After the mumbo-jumbo of the religious cults, here we have the babble of pseudo-personal development. Among many others, a certain John Mitchell maintained, at the end of the 1960s, that Stonehenge was in reality the reproduction of a flying machine observed by men in the Neolithic era![2]

---

[1] See Barbara Marciniak, Bringers of the Dawn: Teachings from the Pleiadians, Bear & Co, 1992.
[2] See John Mitchell, The Flying Saucer Vision: The Holy Grail Restored, Sidgwick Jackson, London, 1967.

The "Pictorial Language" of David Percy

In short, the designs of the crop circles, inevitably "felt" to be extraterrestrial messages and located in the vicinity of ancient megalithic sites, could only inflame imaginations and give rise to esoteric interpretations. The "intelligence" that conceived them, an intelligence that is almost certainly terrestrial rather than extraterrestrial in origin, definitely wanted to play on this connection. And it has certainly succeeded.

The small village of Avebury is located 20 mi. to the north of Stonehenge. This charming Wiltshire settlement would be less well-known if it did not adjoin one of the major sites of terrestrial archeology. Avebury lies at the heart of a gigantic, megalithic infrastructure of standing stones, barrows, wooden temples, avenues, and a giant mound. Its center is an enormous ditch called the "Henge," the biggest, but also one of the least, studied circles in England.

Observing the site, even in its present state, immediate calls to mind the "crazy geniuses" who carried out such a titanic project over 5,000 years ago. The circle (which, from an aerial view resembles a crater) is awesome in its size. It is over 1,150 ft. in diameter and covering 27 acres of ground, with vast external ramparts measuring 53 ft. high, formed by the earth excavated from the 33-ft. deep ditch.

The Megalithic Ditch of Avebury

Nothing is known of the builders of such a marvel, but its construction seems to have predated that of Stonehenge by several centuries. Another part of the complex that is equally impressive is Silbury Hill, a gigantic artificial butte of limestone raised by human effort to a height of 132 ft.

A mysterious satellite "orbiting" a mile from the giant stone circle, this tumulus is the highest man-made feature of prehistoric Europe. And, as in the case of the Avebury circle, the experts have difficulty explaining why it was ever built.

"Titanic" Ditch and Terraced Rampart of the Henge

From Stonehenge and Avebury to the planet Mars is not really just "one small step." But let's take this step for a moment, before returning to the agriglyphs.

Pictures from a region of Mars known as Cydonia Mensae, taken in 1976 by the Viking probe in orbit around the planet, show some rather strange details on the ground. Standing out in the midst of a vast plain is a hill that has justly been nicknamed "The Face." The interplay of shadows and light does give it the appearance of a human face turned to the sky. Other, more recent photos dispel this impression, even though they don't convince those who would rather believe in a NASA cover-up. But to the west of this highly curious artifact,[1] are a number of elements in the form of pyramids. To the east lies a giant crater accompanied by a relatively round butte.

The Author standing in front of Silbury Hill

Now let's return to Earth.

In September 1996, David Percy, who is a photographer and a former European member of "The Mars Mission," a group created in 1983, by Richard Hoagland, to study the mysterious red planet, gave a lecture at the University of Bradford in England on the "mysteries of Mars," and more particularly, on the strange artifacts at Cydonia Mensae. The lecture was titled: "The Terrestrial Connection."

[1] *Whether an ancient shaped object or man-made.*

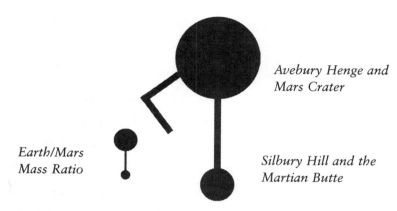

Avebury Henge and
Mars Crater

Earth/Mars
Mass Ratio

Silbury Hill and the
Martian Butte

In his opening remarks, Percy explained how he was struck by an aerial photo of the Avebury site taken from the north. It shows the megalithic circle, with the tumulus of Silbury Hill in the background to the south. "I suppose I had something like a distant reminiscence, I can't explain it otherwise. I said to myself, 'This is what we'd see if we were landing on Mars, close to the constructions. Looking out of the vessel's window, we would see the crater below and, further away, the spiral butte.' It then occurred to me that the terraced rampart and ditch at Avebury could represent the crater, and Silbury Hill, in the distance, the spiral butte on Mars."

In 1991, a pictogram appeared in a field near Silbury Hill.

For Percy, the crop circle schematizes very precisely the megalithic structures at Silbury and Avebury, which are "scale representations of this part of the structures on Mars."

Thus, Avebury Henge, to this inspired photographer, is a reproduction at 1/14th of the scale of the Martian crater. And similarly, the Silbury knoll represents the Cydonia butte. In other words, for Percy, everything indicates that the crop circle is intended to draw attention to this unexpected link. All the more so because the two circles in the lower left of the figure (see diagram) seem to correspond to the relative masses of Earth and Mars. In Percy's view, "someone" wants to draw our attention to Mars.

The Crop Circles Designate Mars!

A simple pictogram drawn in the wheat would thus have helped to resolve an archeological enigma as old as the world. Even the best science fiction screenwriters would not have thought of that.[1]

Let us finish up quickly with this Martian nonsense, especially in light of what one learns about the true personality of Mr. Percy and that of his follower, David Myers. In *The Stargate Conspiracy,* Lynn Picknett and Clive Prince reveal that Percy "belongs to a group of individuals who say they are in contact with extraterrestrials that have attained a very advanced level of development, rendering them akin to gods." Percy and Raël, united? No doubt about it, if one believes these two authors:

[1] *Starting with M. Night Shyamalan, director of the American film, Signs, released in 2002. Shyamalan, who is also the screenwriter, has adopted the view that the crop circles are the work of extraterrestrials wanting to communicate. His hero, a priest who has lost his faith, played by Mel Gibson, is forced to accept the evidence: the lights that haunt the surrounding cornfields are those of the machines responsible for the superb figures visible from the sky. The film, made with a budget of $62 million, remained at the top of the American box office in September 2002. Just to set matters straight, no crop circle has in fact ever appeared in a cornfield.*

Myers and Percy have written a very curious big book, entitled Two-Thirds, *which recounts in fictional fashion the history of our galaxy [...] They (the extraterrestrials) are said to have first colonized Mars (which they rendered habitable, thanks to their sophisticated technology), and built the monuments of Cydonia. Much later, they are said to have debarked on Earth, where they carried out genetic experiments on the natives, over time creating hybrids, the human beings. They are also said to have built at Avebury a counterpart to the Cydonia complex, as well as the Sphinx and the Giza pyramids."*[1]

By linking the major sites in the south of England to the dubious theories put forward by the adepts of a new religion, it is possible that the real authors of the crop circles, instead of taking credit as initiators, might be trying to cover their tracks, helped by "propagandists" like Percy. After having suggested the idea that these extraordinary designs are the work of visitors from space, they then seem to have tossed some decoys to the UFO sleuths. Are Percy and Myers being manipulated or are they accomplices in fraud?

It matters little. Because the analysis of recent agriglyphs will show us that the real designers of the circles, who have camouflaged themselves behind the extraterrestrial thesis while utilizing it to their own advantage, have certainly gone

[1] *Op cit.*

overboard. They have committed some gross errors that help to unmask their deception.

Agriglyphs That Go Too Far

On **August 13, 2000** *(first phase)* — In a field adjoining the enormous radar antenna at the Chilbolton radio telescope complex in Hampshire (20 mi. east of Stonehenge), there appeared a complicated crop circle design, measuring 360 ft. by 230 ft. The strange design was based on several circles of different sizes that seemed to emerge out of one another.[1]

On **August 14, 2001** *(second phase)* — A year later another crop circle was discovered in the same field. For the first time, the complex execution of the design represented a face, which some would call "humanoid." It was conceived with the help of a new texture evoking a "grid" of different sized points (like that of a printed photo). The vague resemblance between the "portrait" and the "Face of Mars" induced certain ufologists to think that a new stage had been reached in the dialogue with an external civilization. What would be the next stage?

On **August 19, 2001** *(third phase)* — A week after the enigmatic face materialized, it was joined by another pattern. This time, the pattern consisted of a response to the radio message sent by the Arecibo observatory in Puerto Rico, a transmission that left on a never-ending journey in 1974.

1 *See photo section.*

At the initiative of the astronomer Francis Drake, father of the famous SETI (Search for Extraterrestrial Intelligence, an attempt to look for extraterrestrial signals) program, a radio message, brainchild of the late Carl Sagan and numerically coded, was sent on November 16, 1974, towards the M13 Great Globular Cluster (350,000 stars near the edge of our galaxy) in the constellation of Hercules. It was transmitted at a power of several million watts for a period of three minutes.

This message, which should be decodable by any civilization in outer space whose level of development is at least equivalent to our own, describes Earth and its technological level in 1974. Conceived in binary code, it is decoded by distributing the "bits," or elementary units, in 73 consecutive groups of 23 characters, and disposing these groups one on top of the other. Inscribed there are the integers "one" to "ten" (our base 10), the atomic numbers of hydrogen, carbon, nitrogen, oxygen, and phosphorus (the principal components of life), the formula for sugars and bases in DNA nucleotides,[1] the number of nucleotides in DNA, the double spiral of DNA, a representation of a human being as well as its size, the population of Earth, the solar system,[2] and lastly, the diameter of the Arecibo radio telescope. In fact, if any answer to this message was forthcoming from the M13 cluster, it would not

---

1 DNA (deoxyribonucleic acid) is formed of two long nucleotide chains twisted into a double helix. Each nucleotide is composed of phosphoric acid, a sugar, and a nitrogen base (A= Adenine, T=Thymine, C=Cytosine, G=Guanine).

2 Earth, designated by a square, is shifted towards the silhouette representing man so that one associates it with the only inhabited planet.

arrive here for at least another 40,000 years (the cluster is located 25,000 light years from Earth.[1]

The agriglyph that was supposed to have responded to this 1974 message merely reproduced the original message but with variants. Among others, the representation of the transmitting telescope, schematized in the 1974 message, was replaced by the design of the crop circle that appeared on August 13 (a multitude of circles). Did that mean "yes, that was us?" The diagram representing our solar system was replaced by another system, also with nine planets,[2] of which three were marked as inhabited, if the message was to be believed. The silhouette of the human being was replaced by a

The initial message, which left Earth in 1974, to which the pictogram near the English radio telescope at Chilbolton is supposed to be a response

smaller figure with an enormous head and big eyes. On a more technical level, the atomic numbers of the principal elements, which are the building blocks of life on Earth, were completed with silicon,[3] while there were notable modifications in the sugars and bases, as well as in the DNA.

---

[1] One light year equals 5,875 billion mi.
[2] What a coincidence! The solar system has nine known planets. The message of the supposed extraterrestrials seems to mean that "their" system has the same number. Unless the real designers simply couldn't be bothered to change the figure.
[3] As it happens, researchers—human ones—have imagined organisms based on silicon... Our pictogram creators seem to read the scientific reviews.

The Chilbolton radio telescope. Access is forbidden to passers-by

Lastly, the population of the enigmatic civilization totals 17 billion individuals.

Is this an extraterrestrial response or a terrestrial maneuver? (Did the alleged extraterrestrials have so little to tell us?) In any case, the SETI Institute, responsible for the extraterrestrial listening program, remains incredulous. On *www.seti.org,* one can read the following remark: "And if they [the extraterrestrials] don't like radio much, they could have left written information, such as a CD."

Almost as if the mysterious designers wanted to show they had visited SETI's Web site, an impressive crop circle, doubtless a follow-up to the Chilbolton formations, materialized a year later, 10 mi. away in a field at Crabwood

Farm House. This design does, in fact, contain the "CD" envisaged by SETI!

On a rectangular surface about 350 ft. by 230 ft. was "printed" an "identity photo" of a strange individual: an enormous head in the form of an inverted pear, almond-shaped eyes, tiny nose and mouth, pointed chin and spindly neck. The evolution in the making of the design brings the face to life with a subtle variation in the size of the horizontal lines, surpassing in beauty, precision, and resolution all of the other crop circles. It is an astounding feat. The circlemakers have certainly perfected their technique and their sense of humor.[1]

But next to the "face," the alien is flanked by a sort of stylized disc around 165 ft. wide, which he is brandishing in his left hand. The interior of this vegetal "CD" contains a spiral groove, obviously conceived in the form of a classic binary code (the small plots of raised and flattened grain configuring either "ones" or "zeros"). It can be translated by applying the international computer code ASCII.[2] Here is the transcription:

Beware the bearer of FALSE gifts and their BROKEN PROMISES. MUCH PAIN but still time. EERIJUE. There is GOOD out there. WE OPpose DECEPTION. Conduit CLOSING (bell sound).

Understand if you can.

---

[1] *See photo section.*

[2] *Each character possesses its translation into numerical code through ASCII (American Standard Code for Information Interchange). Basic ASCII represents characters by seven bits (that is, 128 possible characters, from 0 to 127). For accented languages, like French, ASCII has been extended to eight bits (an octet), enabling the coding of additional characters (extended ASCII).*

Incoherent "Intelligences"

The Chilbolton pictogram that appeared in 2001 as a response to the message sent towards M13 by the Arecibo radio telescope in 1974 has some aberrant features. Even if we pass over the questionable rapidity of the "response" to our "cosmic postcard," it is surprising to see that the general appearance resembles that of man (or rather the image that Hollywood gives them). It is also surprising that the additional atomic element should be silicon. On this point, SETI was not taken in:

We should also note that silicon is now indicated as being partly present in their molecular composition, even though, while popular as a notion in science fiction, this element is fairly poor at constituting the complex molecules required for life.

A civilization capable of traveling in space should possess a level of consciousness and a scientific power that surpasses our understanding. But, what do these "extraordinary intelligences" do in order to communicate with us? They limit themselves (one might say "stupidly") to sending back an unoriginal and uninnovative message, only adding some dubious information.

To try to imbibe the atmosphere of this "opening to the stars," we went to see the Chilbolton radio telescope. What we observed there enabled us to clarify matters.

On a vast private plain closed off by fences, the giant antenna looms, isolated in the middle of the fields but impressive even at a distance of several hundred yards. It is impossible for anyone to venture at night into such a closely watched enclosure to trace out a giant design, which demands lighting and equipment. They would be risking their freedom and possibly their life.

The other message that the pseudo-extraterrestrials are supposed to have delivered at Crabwood, 20 mi. from Chilbolton—the alien bearing his CD-type disc—is also aberrant. Its extraterrestrial physique corresponds, trait by trait, with the archetype that currently holds sway in popular imagination and is conveyed by science fiction films. One is dealing with the famous "Little Gray," who is fond of human abductions and cattle mutilations.[1] But even more serious are the considerable morphological differences visible between the Chilbolton extraterrestrial and this one. It is not the same face. In the space of just one year, there has been an evolution from the "Chilboltonian humanoid" stage in 2001 (which looked fairly similar to a human) to the "Crabwoodian menacing big-brained dwarf" of 2002.

As for the "message" contained on the disc, as abstruse as it may be, it seemed intended to communicate the idea of a hope. But the underlying "psychology" that presided over the

---

[1] For 20 years now, cows, sheep, and horses have been found dead in their pastures, with an organ carefully amputated, as if cut off by a laser. On January 3, 2003, an American newspaper, The Great Fall Tribune (Montana) related a new case of mutilation: "someone" had removed an eye, an ear, and genital parts from a cow. These were carved out precisely, without any trace of steps or activity around the corpse.

conception of this "call" is perplexing. Why talk to us in binary code? Why, given the super-technology used to create the designs in the field, did it not occur to them to speak directly in our own language, or rather the *lingua franca* of English, especially on British soil? Was it a diplomatic stance to avoid offending the sensibilities of non-English speaking peoples?[1] No, these designs decidedly show too much bad "human" logic. Crop circles are not messages from anywhere else, and their true authors have revealed themselves to be quite clumsy in their attempt at manipulation.

It follows, then, that another explanation has to be found for the agriglyphs.

---

[1] *Translator's Note: If that were the case, then why is the message in ASCII code for English alone? They DO in fact speak English, just in a complicated fashion.*

Crop Circles

Chapter Four

A Time for Hoaxes

British rationalists have, at least, invented ecological explanations for the mystery. For its part, the French monthly popular science magazine, *Science & Vie* [Science & Life] felt a duty to offer a serious, and above all, definitive, "reference" thesis to its readers. Because, at *Science & Vie*, what they pejoratively call the "paranormal" and "pseudo-sciences" have no place. To try to resolve the disturbing enigma of the circles in the grain according to accepted rules, *Science & Vie* called upon the services of a research group, VECA, [Voyage d'Etude des Cercles Anglais or English Circles Field Study], made up of eight "skeptics."[1] These French Cartesians spent two weeks in July 1990 in the county of Wiltshire, which they had already visited the previous year. The field study resulted in a report, which in turn inspired an article that appeared in *Science & Vie No. 878*, dated November 1990. While the magazine's article is available to all, the initial report by VECA has, in contrast, remained unknown to the wider public. We obtained a copy, as it was presented at the Rencontres Européennes de Lyon [European Meetings at Lyon], held May 18-20, 1991.

---

[1] *"Skeptic" designates the defender of a rational explanation that owes nothing to the paranormal, magic, or the existence of extraterrestrials on Earth.*

Clearly presented and factual, it is very instructive.

It must be recognized that the VECA group's approach was free of preconceptions. Its report reflects the scale of the phenomenon as well as its major characteristics. The forms of the different figures observed and their evolution from 1980 to 1990 are recorded. Four pages describe the appearance, size, and structure of the circles studied. On this point, the group made several pertinent remarks concerning the general near-perfection of the patterns and confirmed the absence of any damage within the figures, such as uprooted cereal stems. Here is what they wrote concerning the circles themselves:

- The ears of grain were flattened in a regular manner over surfaces ranging from 100 sq. ft. to several thousand sq. ft. (in the form of circles or straight-line segments).
- The transition between the flattened plants and those that remain standing is extremely clear-cut.
- Right angles are well marked.
- A zone of standing ears of grain about a foot in diameter can subsist at the center of a circle.

These are the characteristics of the internal structure:

- The grain was flattened in packets or tufts.
- The tufts followed the regular curve of the figure (concentric circles when the figure was round) with a combed effect.

VECA indicated that these observations were consistent with the use of a roller to flatten the grain (following an experiment we will describe shortly), which strongly implied that human intervention was involved. Towards the end of the report, the study group favored the hypothesis of a clever hoax. The general structure of the flattened areas as well as certain "defects" in fabrication were viewed as the "signature" of fraud.

Before their field study, the researchers had, in June 1990, directed an experiment in full-scale simulation. They asked a special effects expert, André Delepierre, to create a crop circle in a field. The site selected was situated near Verdes, in the Beauce region of France.

In the presence of a bailiff and several members of VECA, armed with a gardener's roller, a stake, rope, and a plan of the figure to be executed, Delepierre entered the field with two assistants at 7 p.m., and emerged an hour later, task completed. The entire experiment took place in full daylight.

VECA member Gilles Durand made several remarks in the report:

A first observation is that the general appearance conformed to that usually described in England. The grain was folded over near to the base, and the system for covering

Delepierre's Method

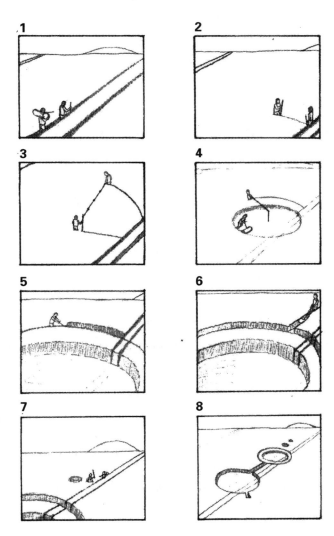

1 – *The operators utilize the tire tracks left by agricultural machinery ("tramlines") to reach the chosen site without leaving prints.*

2 – *A stake is planted at the center of the future circle.*

3 – *A rope tied to a stake allows the perimeter of the circle to be traced.*

4 – *One of the circlemakers uses the roller to flatten the grain inside, while the second traces the perimeter of the ring.*

5 – *The roller is used to widen the ring.*

6 – *Straight lines are made according to the plan.*

7 – *Satellite circles are made thanks to benchmarks already laid down.*

8 – *The figure is ready to convince people to believe in an extraterrestrial message.*

the surface ensured that they were neither broken nor crushed, which was also the case in Great Britain. The central circle presented beyond any doubt the principal characteristics attributed by the British to 'authentic' circles—concentric waves or undulations. Consequently, given all these elements, we can affirm that it is possible, with simple means and a great speed of execution, to construct a crop circle capable of fooling the best experts on the subject.[1]

VECA's official conclusions were more circumspect:

We are in the presence of a phenomenon that, while repetitive, tangible, measurable, and frequent, cannot yet be clearly defined since its nature is diversified [...] One notes the appearance of various types of 'circles' during the course of a single season as well as over the years; why, then, could they not have various origins? [...] Nor does anything exclude, in view of the existing lack of a serious definition of a 'real crop circle' to envisage epiphenomena having different origins.[2]

Even if they tend to support the hoax thesis, the members of the research group recognize that this has not been proven and that a unique solution to the problem remains unlikely. They only report the raw facts, without registering the feelings and opinions of participants. If the demonstration at

---

[1] Frog, 2001
[2] One can consult the site of one VECA member, a "skeptical" but open-minded schoolteacher, Erick Maillot: www.zetetique.ldh.org/agrogrammes.html.

Verdes established that certain circles could be made by men on the ground, it by no means offered categorical proof that such a method was applicable for all of the patterns that have been recorded.

But the article in *Science & Vie,* inspired by the report and signed by Thierry Pindivic, was curiously much less reserved, although Pindivic was himself a VECA member. Isabelle Dumas, also a group member, surprised us with her explanation:

A clarification regarding that article is necessary, because it was distorted by Science & Vie with, in particular, the addition of commentaries that were not the doing of the author. I would cite with respect to this point one most significant passage: 'For quite some time, those who aren't desperately clinging to irrational or para-scientific explanations know that crop circles are quite simply the handiwork of humans. But that has been ignored because the public is in need of the marvelous.' These unexpected additions gave the article a tone that did not reflect the real opinion of the VECA 90 group [...] The article in its published form leaves, in fact, the impression that it sufficed for a team of eight French people to spend two weeks in Great Britain to resolve a mystery on which the English had been working for a whole decade.

What a fine sense of scientific ethics to distort an article in order to present a biased conclusion!

The Case of the "Old Pranksters"

A summer evening in 1978, on a path near Cheesefoot Head in Wiltshire. Two men leave a pub after having gulped down several pints of beer. One of them, who had lived in Australia, told the other about the case of a machine that had landed in a marsh in the state of Queensland,[1] leaving a circular trace among the reeds. And he asked his companion, pointing to a wheat field, whether people would believe the same thing if the two of them flattened the grain there in the form of a circle. Thirteen years later, when the crop circle controversy was reaching a height, this same pair of retired landscape painters (both living in Southampton) stepped into the limelight. Sixty-two-year-old David Chorley and 67-year-old Doug Bower freely admitted that they were the authors of the "hoax of the century." This occurred on September 15, 1991.

Between 1978 and 1991, as a break from routine, they claimed to have jumped the fences surrounding fields while escaping detection by dozens of potential witnesses in order to create *all of the designs*. During these nocturnal outings, they said they "rediscovered their youth" and above all, had a good laugh. They ridiculed the hypotheses raised by the great experts over the previous 13 years. There was no need to

---

[1] *See the case of Tully, Chapter One*

invoke unknown forces or "little green men" to explain the patterns in the fields. Their method was as simple as it was efficient, and the equipment they used was laughable: a small wooden board attached by a cord to an iron stake around which they turned to create the perfect circle.

To support their "confessions," and in front of the television cameras, the elderly pair traced a pattern in less than half an hour. Proof was given. The two retired men from Southampton became famous, the public had its explanation, and the media had a scoop that would make big headlines.

Except, of course, that it was not the end of the story. Doug and Dave were certainly the authors of some designs, but of all the crop circles (even the biggest, as they claimed), certainly not. It is impossible that elderly men could have undertaken such a titanic task in the blackest night, without ever having been detected, shot at by some nervous farmer, or attacked by a guard dog. And to have survived such hard labor!

And finally, was no one astonished that they waited 13 years before revealing themselves and enjoying a certain notoriety? Did no one doubt they could have traveled such distances, each night on English country roads? Southampton is over 25 mi. from the zone of the circles. No, David Chorley and Doug Bower were only occasional circlemakers. The French scientific ufologist, Jacques Vallée, who lives in the United States and is the author of a number of the best documented works on UFOs, was not misled in saying:

What is suspicious about the two older men's 'confession' is that it appeared simultaneously on the front pages of international papers and on CNN the same day. Any published author familiar with the difficulty of getting media attention will know that it takes a very powerful public relations firm to get a story on the front page of the Wall Street Journal, The New York Times, Le Figaro, *and many other papers the same day. Where did the two pensioners get the kind of clout that would spin their claim around the planet?*[1]

It was probably a manipulation. Let's not forget that Doug and Dave's "confessions," on September 15, 1991, curiously followed the appearance, two months earlier, of a crop circle in the form of a cross at the closely watched country residence of the British prime minister. One is justified, then, in wondering if this sudden, liberating "desire for truth," which came at just the right moment to confuse the issue and save John Major from a situation as critical as it was embarrassing, was merely the result of coincidence and the remorse of two old men in their mischievous retirement. Furthermore, little by little, the two accomplices retracted their statements in the years following their initial confession. But it remains the case that they

---

[1] www.chez.com/6sounis/htm/cropvallee2002.htm. *Statement of Jaques Vallée, October 8, 2002.*

contributed to putting a sharp halt to the few serious investigations that the agriglyphs had provoked. Scientists, when they weren't completely discredited, were no longer interested. Public interest also faded rapidly, and each new appearance was considered to be just another hoax.

But something broke down in the scenario that had been carefully constructed around the two retirees' lie. Doug Bowers would state in the *Sunday People* dated December 27, 1998 (Chorley had died in 1996) that he was now convinced that "unknown forces" were in fact at the origin of most of the designs.

Moreover, an important but little-known episode casts a shadow over the whole story of the old pranksters. A serious study carried out by astronomer Gerald Hawkins (respected by his peers for his high degree of scientific rigor and his computer-aided studies of Stonehenge and Nazca), shows the surprisingly complex and well thought-out character of certain agriglyphs. After having closely examined *Circular Evidence,* the book by Delgado and Collins, Hawkins highlighted a fact of prime importance that led him to view the phenomenon from an entirely different angle than that of a vulgar hoax. Certain circles were bearers of a sophisticated "musical code," while others (such as those claimed by Doug and Dave) lacked this feature. To arrive at this astonishing conclusion, the astronomer compared the surface areas of the figures recorded in *Circular Evidence* and discovered that, two times out of three, the ratios between them turned out to be simple fractions, such as 16/3 for some, and 3/2, or 5/3, for others. And all these fractions belonged to the so-called "diatonic" scale, the universal musical code: 16/3 = F, 3/2 = G, 5/3 = A, etc. Out of 18 designs studied, 11 had a precise coding arrangement.[1]

From 1986, when the circles started to be surrounded by rings (as at Cheesefoot Head or Childrey), the arrangement evolved since the elementary fractions corresponded to the surface of the ring divided by that of the circle. The drawings were the work of computer scientists.

Were the pranksters playing an unknown form of music? Were the makers of circles great artists combining a physical feat with mathematical genius? According to Hawkins, "Their intelligence forces our admiration, regardless of what they have done and the manner in which they have proceeded."

The astronomer addressed a letter to the two old hoaxers asking them why they had revealed nothing to the press concerning the high scientific value of their works and how they had proceeded in order to include diatonic functions in them. He never received a reply.

Contradictions Among the Circlemakers

The affair of the "old pranksters" would give birth to a

---

[1] *See* Science News, *October 12, 1996 and* Circles Phenomenon Research International Newsletter, *No. 2 (1997).*

new generation enthused by "Land Art."[1] A generation of artists was motivated by difficult challenges and created ever more complicated designs.

In October 2002, an article in Science & Vie entitled "Crop Circles: How to Make Them" summed up the stakes:

In fact, it was demonstrated, before the eyes of a bailiff, that a gardener's roller placed in the right hands served perfectly well to trace a circle of respectable dimensions in an hour! The mystery was somewhat diminished, but the crop circlemakers, the people who enjoyed creating these very pretty figures in the country, then started to make a name for themselves, profiting from the development of the Internet to exchange experiences, techniques, and plans of forthcoming interventions. The enigmatic people who for several years have been calling themselves "circlemakers"[2] would thus be the prime suspects behind the increasingly complex patterns that have appeared since the two old pranksters gave up the game.

A small number of these "ghosts in the fields" decided to reveal themselves in the full light of day (but most often disguised by carnival masks). Among them were the "artists" John Lundberg, Rod Dickinson, and Wil Russell, who gamely claimed all the large crop circles in England as

---

1 *A movement that appeared in the United States at the end of the 1970s and aimed to produce works at natural sites.*
2 *See:* www.circlemakers.org.

their own. An article in the Scottish newspaper *Daily Record* (September 17, 2002) seemed to verify the whole matter:

The men behind the crop circles yesterday confirmed what we all knew: it was a publicity stunt. And paranormal experts will be gutted to learn Rod Dickinson and John Lundberg have confessed to almost every 'unexplained' crop circle in Britain. [...] Sci-fi enthusiasts maintain the strange formations are proof we are not alone in the universe. But circlemakers admit they make careers out of fooling the public. Dickinson has been sneaking into fields for eleven years and says there is no mystery behind the practice.

He said, "All the big crop circles that have captured people's imagination over the past few years were made by us."

The *Daily Record* also published the confessions of another circlemaker,

It takes meticulous planning. They are designed on a computer and the dimensions are taken into the field with us.[1] The crops are simply flattened with boards. Farmers can pick up everything we flatten so there is no damage at all.

The lucrative side of big publicity coups is perhaps the motivation of these joyful insomniacs who shamelessly violate private property. In 1998, the American TV network

---

[1] *This supposes the use of flashlights to read them and take bearings.*

NBC had the idea of filming a crop circle being made by the hoaxers Dickinson and Lundberg in New Zealand. It was too bad that the figure was destroyed in full haste as soon as it was finished, which of course prevented its examination or the collection of samples. No one was permitted to inspect it.

Concerning this strange experiment, *Science & Vie* simply observed that the circlemakers "even recruited the services of NBC to film and broadcast a documentary on their works, did not hesitate to rent helicopters in order to contemplate their work, and finally, resold their pictures at a high price."

Our "performers" said they utilized their comfortable gains to purchase the logistical means necessary for their nocturnal operations in the fields of southern England. But all this is hardly credible.

First of all, the confessions of these new circlemakers seem to repeat the dubious claims already made by Doug Bower and Dave Chorley, to the point that one might think we had returned to the initial situation, when it was absolutely necessary to calm public opinion. Secondly, the competition has become awkward between all the candidates who, in the last 10 years, have declared themselves to be the sole "Dead Circles Poets." It's difficult to identify the liars among them. A dispatch from Agence France Presse dated November 6, 2000, for example, designated a new, unique circlemaker:

"The mysterious circles, which have appeared regularly these last years in wheat fields of the English countryside, have not been formed by beings from outer space, but, in fact, by humans. Twenty-nine-year-old Matthew Williams, from Wiltshire in the west of England, responsible for this hoax, was arrested with an accomplice and will face trial. For years, these circles have fascinated and intrigued fans of paranormal events. Experts questioned about the phenomenon theorized that the geometric figures which appeared in the early hours of the morning in the fields were due to whirlwinds," etc.

British Coppers Don't Believe It

The cereologist Eltjo Haselhoff, in his book, *The Deepening Complexity of Crop Circles*,[1] reported remarks by circlemaker Dickinson about the method used to create the "Julia Set," a formation that appeared on July 7, 1996 near Stonehenge.

We began with the big central circle, placed just beside a tramline. People have asked us why we made a big central circle, which is slightly offset in a Julia Set. It's simple. To avoid damaging the harvest around the figures, we needed to dispose of a large circular surface, from which we could measure the distances to the other parts of the formation. After having made the first

[1] *Favre, 2002, p. 62*

circle, we determined a work line for the other elements. That's how the spiral was made, by drawing arc sections with the aid of a tape measure from different centers placed inside the first circle. We displaced the centers around the first circle by lengthening the distance for each section of the arc.

Haselhoff counter-attacked:

Despite this apparently well-documented account, the method is false. A simple analysis of an aerial photo suffices to demonstrate that what Dickinson calls the 'work line' could not have been traced from the big central circle [...] In reality, the work line is composed of three circular segments, and only one has its center within the central circle. Contrary to what Dickinson claims, the two others have their center located on a tramline. It is thus incorrect to claim that the entire work line was constructed from the central circle. That is neither a theory nor a supposition. It's a fact. His remark about the manner of drawing the work line from different positions within the central circle even reveals a certain ignorance. As the diameter of the central circle is much smaller than the range of the work line, that would have had no visible effect on the final result. One can conclude that Dickinson was less well informed about his alleged hoax than he'd like to admit.[1]

[1] Op cit.

The whole confessional operation, which suits skeptics, would benefit from synchronizing its actors. The self-confessed circlemakers should agree on who drew what, and above all, how they did so.

But just who was responsible for the impossible crop circle that appeared in front of Prime Minister John Major's country home, which we described above? Curiously, no one came forward to lay claim to this veritable tour de force, which required, at the very least, the collusion of the British secret services.

In November 2002 we went to gather on the spot reactions of the local population; barmen, postal workers, restaurant owners, etc., the British "common people" who are supposed to be fascinated by "their" mysterious circles. Surprisingly, it emerged from our sidewalk interviews that there was a vast ignorance on the subject. If some British people willingly implied, smiling, that an "extraordinary" explanation must be hiding behind the phenomenon, the great majority of people questioned seemed, in effect, to conclude that it was all a hoax.

We asked policemen at Andover, a city located on the border between the two principal counties concerned, Wiltshire and Hampshire, what a "field artist" actually risked. They amiably confided their impressions. First of all, the subject left them indifferent. Secondly, they rejected outright (but with humor) the extraterrestrial thesis. For them, the circles in the wheat were a hoax fabricated by "students" (even though one doesn't see why circlemakers could only be "students"). In response to the question whether they'd ever made any arrests, the police officers said "no." So who was this Matthew Williams of whom the AFP dispatch had spoken? Where was he arrested? The Andover police, for its part, had never officially heard of such an arrest.

But in Great Britain, crop circles are officially no longer a mystery; to the extent that the custodians of the Stonehenge site, like the Andover "bobbies," seem to have received instructions to "deny" the very existence of the designs when this tourist (who had just visited one) asked for their opinion!

Should one thank Doug Bower and Dave Chorley, who will go down in history under the friendly nickname of the "old pranksters," for having, since that famous evening in the pub in 1978, incited vocations and inspired a new generation of artistic mathematicians and geometers? Gathered in various groups, they seem to have taken over from the two retirees with zeal, passion, and interest (even if these young artists do not seem to know very well which designs they did or didn't do). Officially, the immense creations of flattened grain carried out in highly restricted zones are the work of young vandals who belong in prison.

The author, in the company of Michael Glickman (right). The home of this former architect, resembles a crop circle museum.

A Meeting with Michael Glickman

Not everyone shares this opinion, however. The theory that "it's all a hoax" does not stand up to an examination of the situation and the facts. In order to hear a "different tune" than that of the "phantom" circlemakers, who have been such a godsend to rationalists and scientific magazines, we went to listen to the views of a British circle hunter, Michael Glickman.

This kindly retired architect, full of common sense, received us in November 2002 at his home in Wiltshire, near Devizes. It is here, at the heart of "strategic territory," in the green calm of the English countryside, that he has studied the crop circle phenomenon for over 12 years. In his small living room, a veritable "Ali Baba's cavern" of agriglyphs, the walls covered with their photos, from the plainest circles of the 1980s to the latest and most complicated mathematical patterns that appeared the previous summer, we asked him a simple question: "So, is it all a huge hoax?"

In keeping with his very British reserve, Michael did not overly manifest his sense of humor. But his reply was nevertheless quite clear: the thesis of a global hoax, he said, was completely ridiculous and unthinkable. Without equivocating, he accused Doug and Dave of having received financial rewards for their false confession. "They were very certainly paid by 'someone' for discrediting the whole business" (with great success). The two gentlemen were quite incapable at the time, Michael Glickman said, of explaining how they created the most complicated pictograms.

Commenting on the photographs of three different patterns that appeared on the same night (June 23, 1999), he contended that this nocturnal harvest considerably weakened the thesis (currently in fashion) that it was all the work of a few "math students" seeking thrills. To carry out even one of these designs demanded an uncommon physical and mental effort. To succeed in creating three in a row in one night would have been an exploit even for an organized group. But the most telling clue, in his eyes, was the total absence of witnesses. Why had not a single walker, farmer, policeman, or vagabond ever encountered the troop of circlemakers and their equipment, or seen their vehicles and flashlights, during a period lasting over 20 years? Glickman shook his head: "Impossible."

He did not appreciate the attitude of his scientific compatriots, people who were "amputated of their humility and imagination." He deplored their lack of interest in the subject, the total lack of serious studies capable of lifting a corner of the veil. But he did say that one scientist—the only one to find favor in Glickman's eyes—had attempted to do so, a certain Professor Levengood, whose work we will soon present.

Michael Glickman had interviewed some of the farmers who suffered major financial losses from crop circles. The local information that he has gathered is illuminating. The farmers, who are not forthcoming with outsiders, generally speak of a hoax in public, but speak differently when someone local, like Glickman, meets with them privately in the pub. Then many of them soon confided their belief that something mysterious is going on.

Michael is convinced that "unknown forces" are, in fact, at work and responsible for a considerable share of the designs. According to Glickman, only six percent of crop circles that appear are fakes. UFOs? Glickman was ill at ease. Too much nonsense had been said on this subject, he told us. No, it was something else.

We left Michael Glickman's home in the pouring rain, convinced that the circles hid a much more extraordinary truth than impossible hoaxes. A truth that we would have to seek henceforth from the very rare scientists who have questioned the principal "witnesses" of the phenomenon—the ears of wheat themselves.

STATE OF THE "ART"

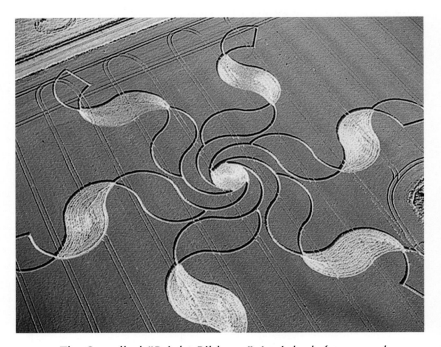

The So-called "Bright Ribbons" Agriglyph (appeared July 4, 2002 near the Megalithic Site of Stonehenge).

This latest generation of crop circles marks the mastery achieved by the "artists" of this new form of Land Art, with diameters on the order of 600 ft. What tools were involved in their making? Surely not just a stake and a rope. All the more strange because it would seem that the complex figures were completed in just a few minutes, without witnesses.

THE "GREAT SPIRAL"

*One of the Most Beautiful "Glyphs" with its
409 Circles (Milk Hill, 2001)*

The biggest circle in this masterpiece measures 70 ft. in diameter. According to the Daily Mail, *a fan of handmade crop circles calculated that a gifted user of the board and the stake would need to draw each circle in under 30 seconds to complete the figure in a single night.*

THE GRAND FINALE

The "Triple Julia Set," Wiltshire (1996)

The "Triple Julia Set" reveals the "mathematical" evolution of the technology at work, the curve is omnipresent, the geometric concept complex. An astronomer, Hawkins, discovered the mathematical formula involved.

"MAGNETIC FIELDS"

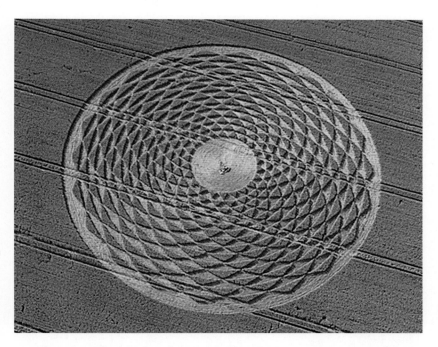

*The So-called "Mandala" Design, Born August 13, 2000
at Woodborough Hill, Wiltshire*

With diameters on the order of 250 ft., examples of crop circle production in 2000 go far beyond the abilities of any "old pranksters." Such a work, always successfully executed in one attempt and apparently on a black night, is not the work of hoaxers.

MAGNETIC FIELDS

"Magnetic Fields," Avebury Trusloe, July 22, 2000, Wiltshire

ENEMY ALIENS

The Crabwood E.T., Summer, 2001

From the year 2000 onwards, the "extraterrestrial" alibi began to appear clearly, just next door to the radio telescope at Chilbolton. But the "face," similar to a human's and rather peaceful (following page), clashes with the caricature of the "Little Gray," drawn a year later, bearing a supposed "message" in binary code. The result is unconvincing. The alien has started to resemble the images of ET.

ENEMY ALIENS

"The Chilbolton Extraterrestrial," August 14, 2000

This sudden break in the artistic "iconography" of the agriglyphs has contributed powerfully to discrediting the "extraterrestrial" thesis, even among spiritualists, quick to believe in the intervention of a benevolent cosmic intelligence.

All the same, these graphic "variants" speak volumes about the mastery of the real "operators."

EVIDENCE OF MANIPULATION

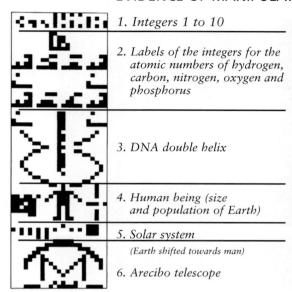

	1. Integers 1 to 10
	2. Labels of the integers for the atomic numbers of hydrogen, carbon, nitrogen, oxygen and phosphorus
	3. DNA double helix
	4. Human being (size and population of Earth)
	5. Solar system
	(Earth shifted towards man)
	6. Arecibo telescope

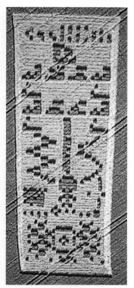

The Coded
Message Sent by
Arecibo in 1974

The "Response"
Drawn in 2001

In 1974, Carl Sagan had the idea of sending a message "on the off chance" to a faraway star cluster, coded in graphic binary code. It gives essential information about the human species intended for an eventual intelligent race. Its designers thus resumed the human story with its number, the atomic weights of the principal components of terrestrial life, etc.

To bolster the extraterrestrial thesis, the anonymous designers of crop circles thought they were being "clever" by drawing in a field, next to the Chilbolton radio telescope, a similar "response." It only had to be decrypted. But the information about the supposed extraterrestrials they included is thoroughly ridiculous. If one is to believe them, the alien designer of the crop circles has a big head on a small body, which should please science fiction fans.

THE ENIGMA'S "NODE"

Here are exclusive documents issued from laboratory tests. The wheat (below) folds at the height of the node nearest to the base of the stem, which collapses under its weight. This observation suffices to distinguish "real" crop circles from handmade ones.

Top: Wheat stems compared before and after treatment. Bottom: Close-up of a small singleton circle.

A REVEALING CLOSE-UP

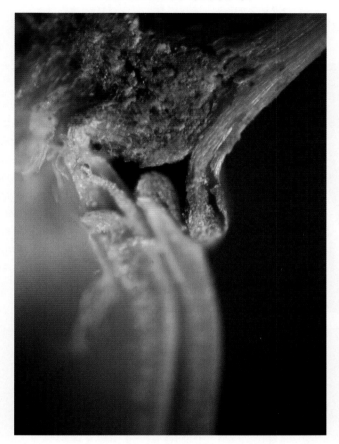

Here is the node of a wheat stem taken from inside a crop circle. It has been completely deprived of its water. A scientist has succeeded in reproducing this effect in the laboratory. By bringing proof of the nature of the energy capable of altering the wheat stem in this way, he held the key to solving the agriglyph enigma.

COMPARISON OF THE TRUE AND THE FALSE

A comparison between two stalks taken from two different designs. The main stem of a "false" crop circle is broken at its base. In contrast, the other stalk has a particular characteristic tied to the "real" phenomenon. The nodes have been bent by "something."

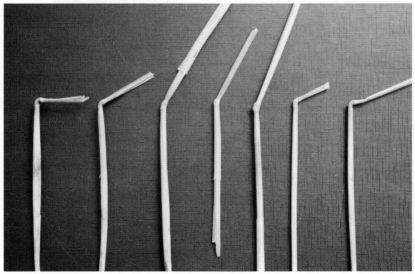

THE KEY TO THE MYSTERY

In a few moments, this potted wheat will collapse

What type of energy will be able to make these wheat plants fold at their base? By discovering this, scientists would understand the terrifying hoax hidden behind the crop circles. At the top of the picture, one can see the laser cannon.

Crop Circles

Chapter Five

Elements of a Serious Investigation

The media, and most scientists who have expressed an opinion on crop circles, use the hoax hypothesis as an "official" thesis. But this does not stand up to scrutiny. We will examine some of the "minor details" that contradict this solution, just as we have ruled out, and hope we have shown why, any "extraterrestrial" thesis. Once the "explanation" that crop circles are the work of pranksters has been invalidated, we can finally examine the first conclusive analysis.

Certain crop circles are, no doubt, gratuitous works of art, nocturnal exploits by whizkids armed with boards, ropes, stakes, and a digital design. And one understands the motivations of these cereal aesthetes: a new exciting form of "Land Art," the expression of a "pure" message, the ancestral need to express oneself on the large-scale canvas of nature, or else the desire to draw attention and win recognition, to dupe people, to pose oneself a challenge, and, probably, to seek financial gain. But these handmade circles do not account for the entire reality behind all of the agriglyphs, in particular the largest, the most sophisticated, and those that occur in fields under close police surveillance.

We know, for example, that it is more than a little difficult to enter English grain fields without drawing attention, especially since the start of the crop circle phenomenon. In October 2000, under a driving rain, we climbed Silbury Hill near Marlborough in Wiltshire, about 130 ft. high, and a site upon which a good number of agriglyphs have appeared. Such an adventure is strictly forbidden, but we wanted to gain a vantage point from which to spot crop figures (even though the wheat, at that time of year, had already been harvested).

Out of breath, we reached the summit of the giant butte after several minutes. Despite a persistent mist and rain that soaked us to the skin, we noticed in a field about 1,000 ft. away the traces of a circle which had a diameter of 330 ft., clearly visible even after the harvest. Our stay on this "Neolithic perch" lasted just long enough to take a few photos. Then we came back down the steep, slippery slope in order to gain access to the field in question. There was not a soul in sight, beyond the continual flow of cars in the distance on the Avebury-Marlborough road.

With some difficulty, we got across a wooden barrier sporting barbed wire and a sign reading "Private Property" (a notion particularly sacred in England) before heading at a run through the mud towards the center of the field where the remnants of the crop circle were still visible.

We stood there for 10 minutes studying the figure and taking photos of the flattened wheat that the harvest had been unable to cut down, before returning to the parking lot and our vehicle. A park warden was waiting for us. With an accusing air, he asked us what we were doing there and warned us that it was forbidden to enter the fields, which constituted a violation of private property. Even worse, he told us in a threatening manner (having obviously been alerted by a phone call) that the farmers, fed up with constant intrusions by tourists, sometimes let their guns do the talking.[1] This little experience demonstrated just how difficult it is (even when it rains) to go about unseen in the fields of the region. At night, the indispensable flashlights (unless the circlemakers wore expensive infrared goggles to pierce the darkness) plus the summertime "surveillance" of tourists, lying in wait in case "something happens," would make any expedition highly risky. And yet despite all that, since the middle of the 1980s, a large number of crop circles continue to appear in the course of the day. Indeed, an anecdote candidly told us by one of the "New Age/cosmic message" cereologists we met shows to what extent the designers operate quickly and invisibly. "We sometimes keep watch throughout the days and nights by shifts," our witness told us. "But it's often just at the moment when the day shift arrives, at the precise moment when no one is watching the

---

[1] *Other witnesses affirmed that some farmers spread toxic substances in the circles to take revenge on invading tourists.*

fields, that the figure appears. We discover it once we resume our surveillance." The alleged "cosmic spirits" have certainly shown themselves to be both careful and facetious.

In reality, it is impossible to work in total secrecy on extremely complex designs, which demand intervention by an entire organized team, with its equipment, ready to activate itself for several hours (the "Julia Set" that appeared on June 7, 1996 in a field near Stonehenge is in that respect, exemplary). But no one has ever seen anything.

Against the reassuring explanation of the gratuitous act, we raise the following points:

- No circlemaker seems to have ever been surprised in the act, but all have left behind a completed work, successfully carried out on the first try perfectly.
- In contrast, all of the "official" demonstrations have always taken place in broad daylight for hours on end, or else at night under artificial light from projectors.
- Some crop circles have necessarily been made with the complicity of certain authorities, since it would have been impossible for ordinary circlemakers to have operated in proximity to John Major's property, the radio telescope at Chilbolton, and elsewhere.

Wheat and Science

Science is the "weapon" that hard-core rationalists

brandish in the face of phenomena that we would describe as "abnormal." We can only applaud such an approach, which guarantees the resolution of many false mysteries. But only on the condition that these same scientists don't decide to punt the ball when the mystery resists analysis.

That's essentially our reproach against *Devenez Sorciers, Devenez Savants,*[1] a popular book written by Georges Charpak, a member of the French Academy of Science, and Henri Broch, a professor at the University of Nice Sophia Antipolis, who holds a chair in "zetetics" (the science of doubt, or skepticism). These two leading scientists affirm that science knows, or can find an answer to, all questions asked. If it can't, they postulate a hoax or conjuring trick is at work. This is indeed the attitude of some authoritative newspapers and magazines (*U.S. News Report* and *Scientific American* in the U.S. and the majority of popular science magazines in France). For them, the mystery of the agriglyphs is limited to a gigantic hoax, on the same scale as the Loch Ness monster or UFOs.

Fortunately, when faced with the evidence, a few scientists have not been content with such simplistic answers. They want to see, touch, and analyze the phenomenon itself.

Among them is the American biophysicist, William C. Levengood, whose work was pointed out to us by Michael

---

[1] *Become Sorcerers, Become Scientists*

Glickman. Not convinced by the facile idea of a hoax that has been spread by the media, this researcher wanted to understand the crop circle phenomenon through a serious study.

Dr. Levengood's Analyses

First of all, Levengood asked himself a sensible question: "Why do the majority of designs appear in cereals and, more particularly, in wheat? Is it a coincidence that this particular plant seems to be favored by the authors of the designs?"

We know that wheat is an annual herbaceous plant of the graminae, or grasses, family (genus Triticum) which produces a caryopsis (grain) from which one makes flour, the main ingredient of bread or pasta. Once its adult state is reached, the plant is characterized by foliar limbs on its stem and an ear carrying 15 spikelets. This stem, long and thin, has several "growth nodes," that resemble small joints. The nodes are in a sense the "ligaments" of the plant that permit it to orient itself towards the light.

The year 1991 marked the explosion in the number of figures in the fields, and the appearance of bigger and more complex patterns, of which the pictograms (including circles, rings, half-rings, "keys," straight lines, triangles) are the most famous examples. It was also the year when crop circles began to be recognizably "exported" to other countries such as the United States, Canada, and Australia.

The British media relayed by the world press pointed scientists and the public toward the thesis of vandals flattening the grain at night (this was when the "Doug and Dave affair" came to light, "deflating" the whole phenomenon).

Dr. Levengood, a respected scientist working at the Pinelandia biophysics laboratory in Michigan, saw, for his part, no objective evidence to support such a hypothesis. His doubts sprang from tests he'd carried out at the end of 1990 on plants taken from the interior of circles in English crops provided by Pat Delgado. And these analyses led him to a surprising observation: the grains of the plants collected in certain fields were smaller than average in size.

In 1992, Nancy Talbott, a former research analyst from Harvard University who had shown an interest for several years in crop circles, accompanied by John Burke, a businessman from New York, offered to assist Levengood in his research and help finance further scientific experiments. For them, it was indeed high time to subject the phenomenon to serious empirical study, free from any preconceptions.

That was how the BLT (Burke, Levengood, Talbott) Research Team was born, based in Massachusetts. The research team, in contact with scientific advisors from various fields, among others analytical chemistry, geochemistry, and geology, developed a scientific protocol for sampling cereals via an organized international network. They undertook a vast study (involving thousands of hours of work spread over several seasons) starting from the complete analysis of the grain collected.

The samples examined came from crop circles in seven different countries (Great Britain, the United States, Canada, Germany, Australia, the Netherlands, and Israel). They were collected at random, from any part of the figures. Each received an identifying number, and its exact position within the formations was carefully recorded. This scientific approach was based upon a solid methodology.

Through this experimental work, William Levengood wanted to see if molecular changes might not have occurred in the plants. Because if such anomalies existed and could be observed, the problem would take on a different light. Indirectly, the circlemakers solution would be invalidated.

The BLT team's initiative was going to be rewarded beyond its hopes. By the end of 1994, samples from 80 geometrical figures had been carefully analyzed (using an electron microscope, infrared spectroscopy, X-ray diffraction, nuclear magnetic resonance, and gas phase chromatography). Levengood detected abnormal physical changes from control samples of ears taken from outside the flattened areas. The principal anatomical alterations concerned the nodes of the cereal, the "ligaments." They showed signs of an astonishing transformation of their cellular structure that was visible to the naked eye: all of the small nodosities had undergone, for an unknown reason, a pronounced elongation.

It seems that this unexplained stretching was the cause of the folding in the lowest node of the stem, the one which supported the entire weight of the ear of grain. This would explain the twisting observed (in most cases at an angle of 45 degrees) and the flattening of the ear of grain.

More than 90 percent of the samples analyzed (hardly negligible) revealed this deviancy. "Something" seemed to have acted on the structure of the plants that led to their tipping over. What could it be?

Levengood also observed that certain nodes affected by this curious phenomenon presented "expulsion cavities," small orifices caused by pressure from the heating of internal humidity. This important clue proves that the plant was subjected to brief but intense heat, deforming them and dilating their bulbs, even to the point of explosion.

Being a good scientist, the biophysicist did not neglect to seek natural causes, already documented, which might explain these peculiarities, only to dismiss them quickly: excessive fertilization, the resistance of wheat to lack of gravity ("gravitropism") or its natural tendency to re-orient

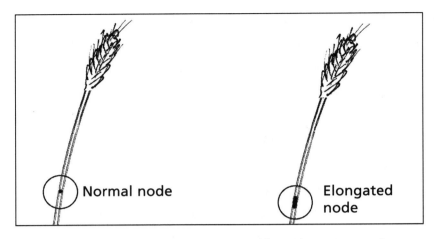

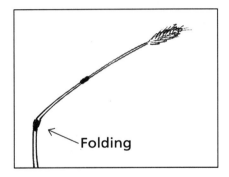

itself to the sun are factors that do not provoke the anomalies observed. All of this did not prevent critics from writing:

The stems of wheat that present a small hole in the node of the plant were sampled by Dr. Levengood. The laboratory analyses lead one to think that these holes were caused by the plant drying out, causing an implosion or explosion. The problem, there again, is that among the 'real' crop circles, few samples have this anomaly.[1] Some cases were found, to be sure, but not systematically. This discovery is therefore not very

---

[1] *Author's note: on what basis is this claim made?*

significant and does not prove in any way the non-human origin of the circles in the wheat. It is highly probable, moreover, that one also finds these nodes with holes in the rest of the field and that these have a natural origin[1]. If not, one could say that the flattened, damaged wheat dried out due to the lack of rising sap, and that it exploded under the effect of the sun's heat.[2]

It's also obvious that nothing that was observed in the cereal nodes could have been induced, in any manner, by the circlemakers' technique, using a wooden board or a roller.[3]

The Grains, Too

Using the same protocol, BLT carried out an in-depth study of grains taken from the ears found within the crop circles. Submitted to analysis conceived to compare their development with control samples, the grains revealed two additional surprises: an abnormal mutation, apparently variable according to the plant species in question, and modifications in their development at the moment when the figure appeared. The growth and germination of some ears suffered a delay, but other grains, sampled from plants that had already ripened when the circles appeared, show a massive increase in their growth rate and vigor. The plants that were "stimulated" in this manner showed a greater resistance than others to lack of light or water.

---

[1] *Author's note: a second "gratuitous" assertion.*
[2] http://site.voila.fr/cropcircle.critique/page7.html
[3] *This is the essential criteria that distinguishes the circles made by pranksters from the others: the author has sampled intact stems taken from the interior of the circles, that have been simply flattened, but he has also found stems in other circles that have been mechanically crushed.*

What happened? If the ears really were exposed to strong heat, why weren't they burnt up in their entirety?

Since 1994, more than 300 agriglyphs were analyzed and the results accumulated (they in fact provided material for three scientific papers published in 1994, 1995, and 1999).[1] They provided other measurements confirming that the vast majority of crop circles that had appeared in fields both in England and other countries (in much more reduced numbers), had plants presenting abnormal features, which were well defined and scientifically measurable: these refuted the thesis of a hoax using "board, rope, and stake."

In 1999, Levengood and Talbott published their most recent conclusions in *Physiologia Plantarum,* an international publication of the Sociétés Européennes de Physiologie des Plantes [European Societies of Plant Physiology] – whom one can consult via *www.fgk.org,* the site maintained by the GACCR, (or German Association for Crop Circle Research). The fruit of meticulous research carried out over 10 years, these conclusions exclude human manipulations on the ground and lend support to the idea that "external energies" capable of forming crop circles were employed, without manual intervention at the site. These energies produced an intense, instantaneous heating of the vegetal tissues of the plants. Over 90 percent of the samples examined had the anomalies described by Dr. Levengood.

---

[1] *Levengood, W.C., Anatomical Anomalies in Crop Formation Plants, Physiologia Plantarum, 1994; W.C. Levengood & John A. Burke (1995), Semi-Molten Meteoric Iron Associated with a Crop Formation, Journal of Scientific Exploration; W.C. Levengood & Nancy P. Talbott, (1999), Dispersion of energies in worldwide crop formations, Physiologia Plantarum, 1999.*

In 2001, the biophysicist carried out more samplings, notably in the impressive crop formation covering 12 acres and composed of 409 circles, discovered on Sunday, August 12 of that year on the Milk Hill plateau in Wiltshire. Again, he observed an elongation of their nodes, affected by "expulsion cavities" (minuscule orifices).

Levengood also noted that the weight of the grains in the ears of cereal taken from within the crop circles was inferior to the average but that their average rate of growth was over five times higher than that of normal grains (a paradoxical result). Contacted, Nancy Talbott amiably directed us to the BLT Web site, where one can see experiments, notes, reports, and photographs of plants taken from the circles, with their particularities. We invite readers to consult these scientific documents, freely available at *www.bltresearch.com* to draw their own conclusions.

The results obtained by Levengood and BLT are unambiguous. "Something" acted directly on the molecular structure of the cereal, and specifically on the nodes, to twist the stems and induce an overall movement. We need only to discover what this "something" might be.

Crop Circles

Chapter Six

The Enigma's Node

Was Dr. Levengood really the only scientist to have taken the trouble to examine the flattened grain in British fields? It seemed unthinkable to us. With the help of the Internet, we therefore attempted to find scientists who, throughout the world, had no doubt also procured some sheaves of flattened grain. But even the most specialized search engines came up empty. There was no one. Nor did we come across anything in scientific reviews. Evidently, the explanation along the lines of "a quick raid on the wheat and back out" had satisfied most of the journalists, whether working in TV, radio, print, or online, and was enough to close the case file.

We tried our best, helped by the grapevine and luck. When the telephone rang, one spring morning, we weren't expecting that it would be the prelude to a meeting with exactly the kind of person we were looking for. And even less that he would be a fellow Frenchman. At the other end of the line, a journalist friend said that he knew, perhaps, a promising informant.

I know this person from having met him at a conference. We got into a lengthy discussion about some ideas concerning the subject you're interested in. I don't know where he is right now, you have to understand that his anonymity is imperative. I'm counting on your sense of discretion.

Anonymity? A French scientist? Concerning certain closely guarded topics, our researchers in France have to put on a burka when dealing with the media. The friend who put us in touch has no idea how much our investigation owes to him. The man we contacted through his good services is an engineer employed by a big military research establishment located in the Paris region. He explained that he could not involve or commit the French defense agency for which he worked by revealing his identity. He was ready, however, to give us his thoughts about the "CC," as he tended to refer to crop circles out of a reflex habit designed to preserve discretion. And he authorized us to reveal the conclusion of capital importance which he had reached after analyzing the problem for a decade. Indeed, as he told us, he had "a global and coherent answer to understanding this enigma."

Until our meeting with him, we had difficulty believing in this heaven-sent gift. Yet, right from the start, our anonymous engineer affirmed to us that his "discovery" addressed in a rational and scientific fashion all of the questions raised by the agriglyphs.

We asked him if the French civilian and military authorities sponsored his research.

No. When I started to gather together my observations at the end of the 1980s the French authorities were completely unaware of what might lie hidden behind the crop circles.

The freedom of action that his investigations permitted him gave him access to the technical means and laboratory analyses needed to verify his working hypotheses. Monsieur X explained to us that he'd been to England several times to visit the "CC" sites. And it was there that he became aware of the scale of the problem. His collection of clues and evidence gave him the keys to understanding the mystery.

We are going to communicate these "keys" just as we received them. We ask readers not to regard the anonymity of our "deep throat" as devaluing, in any way, the quality of his reasoning or the credibility of our approach. You will be able to judge that for yourselves, after having been apprised of the import of Monsieur X's conclusions, and will understand why it is impossible for us to reveal his identity.

For convenience sake, hereafter, we will give Monsieur X the pseudonym of Jean-Paul Piton. We have preferred to render in the form of dialogue the essence of the interview he granted to us that day, at his home in the Paris suburbs.

• • •

Jean-Paul Piton:

Towards the end of the 1980s, when people were starting to talk about these strange circles appearing in the fields of southern England, like many people, I observed it with an amused, if circumspect, gaze.

It wasn't until the phenomenon became recurrent, when the media coverage went beyond the British national scene to become international in scope, that I understood that this business was not as quaintly bizarre as the newspapers were making out. It was even curious to see that such a small news item could run so long, with the great big Hollywood production, Signs, *that was just released at the end of last year, providing a final resounding note.*

In fact, it was quite simply curiosity and my desire to understand what was going on over there, right next door to us here in France, when nothing of a similar nature was being found in our own cereal fields, that incited me to pay closer attention to these events. But it wasn't only that. Professionally, I'd carried out over a period of 20 years investigations for an audit and security service concerned with aeronautical accidents within the French Ministry of the Air Force. Then I was in charge of a materials testing laboratory within a military establishment here in the Paris region. On many occasions, my work involved long and difficult, even painful, investigations, where I had to sort out seemingly inextricable tangles. Only science and technical know-how permitted these enigmas to be resolved.

What made you realize that this phenomenon was not as simple as it seemed at first sight?

Jean-Paul Piton:

It was little things at first, minor details, but ones that revealed a whole other dimension that did not correspond with reality. As if there was something else that lay hidden behind all that. To give you one example: the lack of any reaction from the official authorities in Her Gracious Majesty's realm. Or even the inertia shown by the actors most closely concerned—the farmers. For years, hundreds of farmers watched as their fields were 'splashed' with innumerable designs; very decorative ones, to be sure, but nevertheless totally unproductive from an economic point of view.

The arrival of hordes of curiosity seekers who trampled and devastated their fields whenever even the smallest 'agriglyph' was spotted should have aroused some reaction. Can you imagine the same scenario happening in the French countryside? We would have had peasant demonstrations with roadblocks! Alright, I'm just kidding, there were in fact some reactions in England. Some farmers, a little cleverer than others, found a way to make hay out of wheat. They made visitors pay for the right to enter their 'decorated' field. There was even one farmer who placed a trailer at the end of the path and not only demanded an entry fee, with tickets, but offered T-shirts for sale with a print of the pictogram in his field!

I therefore sought to impose a little order, method, and common sense in all this, by thinking about the angle by which the subject should be approached. Quite simply as a way to avoid the easy pitfall of those who already brought the answers with them before having confronted the facts of the problem.

That's an elementary rule that any investigator, scientific researcher or not, should follow. In school, a teacher used to put it to us more simply: 'Let's present ourselves the problem.' He meant: 'What's it about? Where is it happening? When did it take place? How is it made? With what tools or means does one reach this result?' etc. It's only at the moment when I have succeeded in getting enough answers concerning the duly established and verified facts, and only at that precise stage, that I will be able to elaborate a global hypothesis.

Next, I'll verify whether this is 'irrefutable,' to use scientific jargon, meaning that on my own I can find no way to reject it out of hand. That's the reason I would like to get to the essence and indicate to you the major point that allowed me to elaborate on this theory.

Let's go back to the beginning. The first objective fact I observed is that the phenomenon has been repeated each year for over two decades now in the cereal fields of southern England. The basic, elementary figure is always a small-sized circle, even in the case of the most vast and complex sets. In fact, it's from that the expression used by the experts is derived: 'crop circles,' circles in the crops. But most of the agriglyphs are not very often visible in their entirety except by gaining height in order to observe them, by rising above ground level.

An essential element, and we'll later see its importance, is the nature of the vegetation. Those responsible for these designs no longer use anything but wheat as a support for 'CCs.'

In the very beginning, one did see figures created at the expense of rapeseed plants. Several attempts were aborted in alfalfa fields. But very quickly, only wheat *became the target of designs. From then on, a notable evolution in the complexity of the figures over time becomes apparent. Starting with single circles, the 'CCs' have today become veritable works of art for some people, like the famous pictogram at Chilbolton.*

The second question concerns the zone and the places where these famous circles are situated. They occur essentially in England, and more precisely, in the counties of Wiltshire and Hampshire. When one finds them elsewhere, they are just a few isolated cases, not really comparable to the 'real English CCs.' The working hypothesis that I retained consisted in only taking into account pictograms with an English 'quality label,' so to speak, and more precisely, originating in southern England.

But why was it that in this southern zone of England crop circles grew like daisies in the meadows? At this point, I examined all the geographical, historical, cultural, and sociological factors to discover in what ways this region was different from others. The south of England has nothing to distinguish it, at first sight, from other wheat-producing regions. The only differences are the great concentration of archeological vestiges and the great amount of land classified as 'military zones,' although I should point out that, at that stage, I barely knew anything about the second of these.

Next, analytical logic demanded that I examine another aspect—the period when the designs appear. This is just before the start of harvests, at the very moment when the wheat is reaching maturity when the color changes from green to yellow but the ears are not yet ripe enough to be reaped. Another observation is that crop circles do not appear at the height of summer, when the harvest is at a peak, and both the ears and stems have turned dry and straw-colored.

The period of the year seems to be a determinant factor. It's one of the points that would turn out to be of major importance. And it was through this observation that I understood why wheat was the only form of vegetation involved in this business.

To the best of my knowledge, and a further key element, was that no direct witness has ever seen the formation of a design, from the very beginning right up until today. Why was that? Because the circles were only produced at night? Or because they were carried out from a distance? I confess that at that time I was very much incapable of providing answers to these questions."

You haven't talked yet about the evolution of the agriglyphs themselves, over ten years.

Jean-Paul Piton:

I'm coming to that. If one examines the development of the figures and designs in the English wheat fields attentively, from the very start, several elements show that the size, 20 years over, and the forms and the complexity of the agriglyphs, since 1990, have evolved considerably. The basic, elementary form still remains a circle, whose minimum size is from between 8 and 12 inches in diameter. A second point is that, during the first 12 years prior to 1990, only circles and rings appeared, whose diameter varied, up to several tens of feet for the biggest.

Visiting the sites, I noticed one detail that has escaped mention: the round spaces are not always perfect circles in geometrical terms but ellipses when they're on land that isn't horizontal! This seemingly minor detail will be of critical importance for the rest of my argument about the origin of these strange shapes in the grain.

What makes you think 1990 was a turning point?
Jean-Paul Piton:

It was at Alton Barnes in July 1990 that the first veritable 'pictogram' appeared. This was the beginning of a series that has not been interrupted since. It made the front pages of the newspapers at the time, with its 410 ft. length, and its succession of rectangular and round segments. From year to year, the pictograms have multiplied. But, above all, it's the designs that have struck me, because the forms have become more and more varied, complex, and suggestive. The apotheosis, if I may say so, remains Chilbolton, one of the strangest pictorial and symbolic works I've ever seen.

That's true, but is there nothing that indicates that not just anybody could draw such figures in the wheat fields, either in England or elsewhere?

Jean-Paul Piton:

You're right, but it's precisely at that moment that things get interesting in terms of analyzing the phenomenon. Up to now, we have examined only the external visual aspects of circles, at the scale of the whole cultural system, the geographical system, the geometry of the figure, etc.

But if the outward appearance of the phenomenon did not tell me much that would allow me to form an opinion about the agriglyphs, then I needed to look at the elements most directly associated with "CCs"—the soil and the cereal—in a much more detailed and precise fashion.

As for the soils, I studied their location, their nature, their composition, but also the way in which they had been worked over. I made on-the-spot visits in various counties, gathered information, consulted the local agricultural bodies, questioned farmers about the nature of the soils, the methods of farming, the seeds that had been used, the fertilizers employed, etc. And, of course, I brought back to France samples of English earth (from several plots, located in different regions).

The analyses that came back to me from the lab showed no differences at all between soil to which 'CCs' have been traced and those where nothing has happened. One could therefore dismiss the idea that a substance had been directly spread on the ground.

If you haven't found anything in particular either about the cereal-growing areas of southern England or in the soil and its environment, then what other factors are likely to be at the bottom of all this?

Jean-Paul Piton:

The only element that had never been mentioned by any cereological researcher was the nature of the wheat itself. Observing whether the structure had been modified by something biological or not that would act directly or indirectly upon the plants. One detail that struck me as curious when I found myself inside a circle, looking at the interface was that the border between the design and the wheat outside, was a relatively clear-cut interface and there was no 'edge' effect, like a stain on blotting paper, for example. That meant there was a targeted and homogeneous transition between the design and the wheat outside.

And that also meant that, in order to create such neat contours, especially in the large, complex 'pictograms,' one needed to dispose of an external system capable of acting upon each and every ear of grain. To verify this, the only method is to take on-the-spot samples of the wheat within and outside the agriglyphs, as quickly as possible after the circle first appears. That is what I started to do, from the beginning of the 1990 crop circle season.

Tracking down the first circles, I hurried out into the fields, as discreetly as I could manage, like an impatient fisherman or hunter at the season's opening. At that time, there was hardly anybody out there, and the fields were much more accessible than today. Equipped with everything the perfect wheat hunter requires, I thus ventured into the fields at daybreak, when I knew that only chickens and farmers were up and about, to gather my own personal harvest. According to a protocol worked out beforehand with a laboratory specialized in this domain, I systematically took samples of wheat with both the stem and the ear from inside and outside of *each spot where I found an interesting 'CC' to examine. Upon returning to France, I rapidly contacted biochemical testing laboratories to have them examine biological differences in these freshly gathered samples.*

The results came back to me. I was expecting to find something highlighting a disturbing effect. Nothing. There was no virus, no bacterium, or other pathological agent capable of flattening the ears. Therefore only one possibility remained: a very specific physical effect acting on the very structure of the plants. But why wheat? I needed to find out.

We have seen that only wheat fields are "touched" by the agriglyph phenomenon. But at the beginning of this whole affair, in Circular Evidence, *the book written by Pat Delgado and Colin Andrews, they alluded to (with photographic evidence) figures that had been constituted in clover, rapeseed, and even other cereals such as barley. But it was wheat, in the end, that attracted the designs. Wheat must therefore have had particular features that are propitious to making pictograms.*

An attentive examination of wheat plants in each crop circle and especially of the stems, shows that on each one there was systematically a fold at the node closest to the ground, and no breakage at all of the stem. This is fundamental to understanding the process through which each plant is bent, how it is flattened near to the ground. When you try to fold a wheat stem by hand, you find that the stem, beyond a certain elastic limit, is going to snap by breakage of the tube's fibers. But inside the circles, the stems are never broken.

The central node of the problems is in fact these nodes.

Or to be more precise, the folds in the nodes, particularly those that are closest to the ground. Visual examination confirms that it's there, in fact, that the plants are bent. A cross-section produced at the lab shows that the fold is comparable to tissue that retracts in a joint without any rupture of the fiber.[1] Once the retraction has been engaged on the node, there is no way for the stem to spring back upright, it has been definitively bent over. Like when plastic is heat-injected into a mold. As it cools, it keeps the mold's shape. What is it that might only act on this part of the plant, without altering the thin stem at the end of which one finds the head of the ear?

It's here that science becomes highly useful because we have both the indisputable, if not unignorable, fact that the wheat is bent at the first node, and numerous other pieces of information that 'delimit' the equation to be solved. It's often said that the scientific fact, in order

---

[1] *cf. photo section*

to be validated, must be reproducible. In this case, if we could reproduce the same phenomenon elsewhere, if possible in the lab, then we could thus complete this step in our argument explaining the 'CC' phenomenon.

You thus went and produced agriglyphs in the laboratory? Jean-Paul Piton:

In a sense. The idea came to me to subject ears of wheat to electromagnetic force fields in order to test their reactions. I asked an agronomical laboratory to grow wheat in pots during the winter of 1991-92. At the end of spring, when the wheat had reached maturity, I went to fetch my pots in order to carry out my experiments. I should imagine that the technician in charge of this task must still be asking himself, 10 years later, what those pots were for.

I wanted to quickly test the hypothesis of an electromagnetic force field. The experiment was carried out in a laboratory equipped with powerful lasers, which alone could deliver enough energy to act on the structures of the ears of wheat. I wasn't intervening by chance, because this idea of provoking a thermal effect by a powerful electromagnetic force occurred to me following the negative results from tests on the soil and biochemical analyses of the vegetation. All the biochemical tests, except those of the rate of humidity retention by the ears, had produced nothing. However, the level of water contained in the ears was 50 times lower than that found in plants taken from outside the 'CCs.'

I had also, and this is anecdotal, tried something similar several days earlier in a field near my home where wheat was growing, using very crude, ridiculous means. I lay on the ground, keeping a hair dryer fed by a long electric cable pointed at the wheat for several minutes, trying to provoke the supposed effect that would bend the ears. Of course, I managed to obtain no such thing.

Our lab experiment, with the laser, was in contrast rather delicate to execute, insofar as the lasers in question were tested on the armor of tanks rather than on fragile plants. Imagine the faces of the technicians when they had to adjust the machine's settings. In fact, I wanted to demonstrate two things: that an important thermal effect created by a laser could provoke a visible reaction on the plant's structure; and if possible, produce the bending or something similar in the nodes of ears of wheat.

The experiment was carried with the pots of wheat positioned and inclined at a 45 degree angle under an infrared laser eight inches in diameter. Since we had no references, we operated at varying times and power settings[1] The first firings proved catastrophic for the wheat! The power was much too high and completely disintegrated the plants. Other experiments showed absolutely no apparent effect on the samples.

After all these fruitless tests, and when there were only two or three pots left, we decided with the technicians to reduce the laser power to a minimum, and only vary the duration of exposure. It was at that stage we observed that a duration of nearly 60 seconds gave us something interesting.

During the test, I had seen that the leaves and stems had twisted slightly. Given the low level of my remaining stock, I repeated the experiment with the last two pots, this time increasing the length of exposure. I finally obtained something that resembled a bending of the nodes. The 45 degree inclination of the pot made the plant act like a lever, and distinctly bent the first node.

Is that what bent the wheat in the crop circles, a laser beam? Jean-Paul Piton:

An electromagnetic beam, at any rate. It still remains to be determined precisely what frequency band was used, and the nature of the system deployed to draw pictures on the ground. Whatever the type of radiation

---

[1] *A maser is a laser adapted to magnify microwaves (Microwave Amplification by Simulated Emission of Radiation).*

involved, it's clear that it was a thermal effect, by radiation, that provoked this alteration in the plants.

But the laser completely destroyed the ears of wheat. After queries to plant experts, I realized that the beam we tested operated in the infrared range, which only allows a penetration of a few microns beneath the plant's skin. That is insufficient to set up a thermal flux inside the tissues. I therefore had to turn towards microwaves and masers[1] for answers to my questions. So I repeated the experiment with microwaves and the wheat collapsed, just like in the crop circles.

Why microwaves?

Jean-Paul Piton:

The reason is a simple one everybody can understand. The field of applications for microwaves in its military and civilian development has become very widespread and generalized. Today, who could take an airplane without being tracked by radar? Who hasn't reheated frozen food in a microwave oven? These two instruments have one point in common, they employ the same principle: the emission of an electromagnetic field in the ultrahigh frequency range.

In the case of radar, the emission field is used to bounce back from a target in order to detect and track it.

In the case of a microwave oven, it's the opposite: the radiation penetrates inside tissue, and it's the reverse in direction of the microwave electrical field, thousands of times per second, that results in the agitation of the water molecules present in biological cells and generates a thermal cooking effect.

But how does one go from a microwave oven to these designs in the wheat fields?

Jean-Paul Piton:

If we send packets of microwaves by successive pulses at very high power, megawatts or gigawatts, for very short periods, we dispose of a weak but sufficient energy to alter the ears of wheat. The water contained in the most important part of the stem, the node, is instantly vaporized. The heat convection from the ground adds to the heat caused by the direct flux. The water, which represents 90 to 95 percent of the matter constituting the ear of wheat, will almost reach boiling point within the stem and the node. The node contains a lot of cellulose engorged with water. And like a caramel being heated, it goes soft and becomes deformed until finally, under the weight of the whole ear, it collapses by folding inwards, at the lower level. This is the phenomenon that we see clearly even in macroscopic photos of node cross-sections in plants taken from inside the circles.

I understand about the microwave beams. But how is the flux controlled to draw figures from a distance?

Jean-Paul Piton:

It's there that we have to return to the beginning of the whole affair by examining not just the wheat plants themselves but the most elementary surface in the design, the small-sized circle of a few dozen inches. This small-sized circle is used to generate the entire construction of the figures. It's essential, because even when one finds squares, rectangles, or other forms composing the glyphs, no right angle is made without an arc of a circle on each of their sides.

Similarly, I've observed that when the land is sloped, the circles were no longer perfectly round, but elliptical. In other words, the circles were sectioned by an oblique plane, which indicates the probable spatial origin of the source producing them. Thus, crop circles are, in my view, probably created from the sky above. The simplest method is to emit a microwave beam from an airborne system and draw the agriglyphs on the ground below.

You mean that people have been amusing themselves for years by drawing graffiti from the sky? But who, what, and why?

Jean-Paul Piton:

I think that the system that has been utilized for over a decade includes several elements whose technology has evolved over time. Let's say right away that in order to deploy such systems, one needs enormous technical, financial, and logistical resources. That removes from this hypothesis any type of private initiative. Only public, military institutional structures could have such a capacity.

In practice, one would need to possess an HPM, which means a 'High-Powered Microwave.' It's a sort of cannon, with a head, embarked on a platform with a source of energy supplying several megawatts, or even gigawatts, continuously to feed the HPM generator. But the greatest difficulty involves the stability and piloting of the platform for the instrument and the HPM generator. If you bring together those three elements, however, then you can draw agriglyphs in the wheat fields.

So what you are telling us is that the British state, through its army, has probably been testing for the last twenty years, in the greatest secrecy, a weapon that is a type of high-powered microwave cannon, by creating increasingly refined designs in the wheat fields within its own territory?

Jean-Paul Piton: "That is exactly the conclusion I reached."

• • •

After having "digested" this revelation, we took up, in the company of Jean-Paul Piton, one after another, each of the different elements supporting his hypothesis.

– The HPM generator is available today and has probably already been utilized by certain countries in both civilian and military applications. It should not be forgotten, either, that the British invented radar and were the first to use it during the Second World War. The only major technological innovation involved in this new development was no doubt the perfection of an HPM generator capable of producing a beam in the form of a "paintbrush" that can be moved along two axes to create the "drawing." This advance probably occurred in 1990, when the rings began to appear, followed by the pictograms such as the one at Alton Barnes.

– The platform that carries the HPM must also contain the generator and furnish the electrical power necessary for the generator's operation. There are several possibilities. Either the HPM is the only heavy piece of equipment aboard the stabilized platform, and receives its energy directly from the ground via a transfer system—which may itself involve microwave transmissions, for example. Or else the HPM, the electrical generator, and the platform form a single unit, in the form of an airplane or a dirigible balloon. Our informant leaned towards the latter solution as the best compromise for this kind of system.

– Unquestionably, the known conditions under which agriglyphs are created all "fit" with this set-up: the absence of witnesses, the fact that they appear at night, and the fact that the platform can even stabilize itself over a layer a clouds. This is ideal, for example, in the case of a dirigible.

– Lastly, sites and places selected for laying out pictograms are by no means random. They are centered on a zone only a few dozen miles wide, surrounded by some of biggest military bases in Great Britain, in particular the Royal Air Force base at Boscombe Down Air Field. Precision in the "firing range" plays, in effect, an important role, because an error of even a few meters could provoke a serious risk. Which would lead to the probable use of a system like GPS,[1] a good survey map upon which one would meticulously determine the target, and a computer, of course, by which one would program both the location of the sites and the diagrams of the crop circles that the emitting head would draw. Once they were hit, the wheat stems would collapse in a few seconds, regardless of whether it was rainy or foggy.

Added to this set of arguments is a testimony which lends powerful support in a backhanded manner to the scenario defended by Jean-Paul Piton. It comes from a cereologist convinced that crop circles are magical messages from the

---

[1] *Global Positioning System, a navigation aid based on a network of satellites emitting radio signals. A mobile unit equipped with GPS can determine its position with precision at any hour, from anywhere, regardless of weather conditions. For the military, a point can be located thanks to GPS to within a distance of 10 meters (but over 50 meters for civilian applications). It is controlled by the American Department of Defense.*

[2] *"The Mysterious Crop Circles: Language of the Earth, Expression of the Universe," lecture given on January 31, 2003 in Paris.*

"Earth Mother."[2] One day she spotted a crop circle that had, exceptionally, been created in a field of barley, rather than wheat. She entered it and took some close-up photographs of the cereal stems. She noticed (and this was visible in her picture) that the barley plants had not folded at the base like wheat did: the stems had simply collapse at about mid-height. This shows, first of all, that this was not a hoax perpetrated by "old pranksters" (their roller or board would have broken or folded the barley in the same fashion as wheat). And secondly, that the microwave beam does not affect barley in the same way as wheat, quite simply because the nodes on the stems of the two types of cereals are not distributed in the same manner.

By the way, the cereologist in question confessed her difficulty in understanding why the "cosmic intelligence" that was drawing in the fields did not know how to flatten barley as it did in the case of wheat.

• • •

So, you think that it's the British military which is behind these circles?

Jean-Paul Piton:

I don't see any other authority capable of operating in this way in the English sky.

But our British neighbors are sensible people, and the

British army is led by responsible officers. How are we to make any sense of this game that is now over 20 years old, of the fake messages from extraterrestrials, of these fractals that disturb Her Majesty's farmers?

Jean-Paul Piton:

That's a question to which I will not give you an immediate answer because it goes beyond the purely scientific and technical framework. But you can well imagine that it's not simply a game. It is certainly a military game, but one that has been perfectly thought out and orchestrated.

Chapter Seven

The Arms They Are Hiding From Us

Has the whole story been told?

"Jean-Paul Piton" is a well-known and respected French scientist. Has he elucidated, through his field trips, samplings, experiments, and rigorous reasoning, the enigma of the pictograms drawn in the wheat of the English countryside for more than 20 years? And done so despite not being able to reveal his solution in the full light of day?

We have good reason to believe him if only because we have observed the extraordinary convergence between the only serious research carried out in the field by two scientists who do not know one another, who have never communicated with one another, but whose conclusions tally because they have both taken pains to pursue a rigorous scientific approach: the American William Levengood and a Frenchman who remains anonymous for now, hidden behind the pseudonym of Jean-Paul Piton.

But questions remain. Are the British military experimenting, under the noses of the entire world (including British civil society) with a new offensive or defensive weapon? Are they obliged, given the military stakes, to carry out their tests on an ever-increasing scale, tests that would be impossible to conduct in deep secrecy on its own lands—if only because they are devoid of wheat? Has the military leadership, with or without the consent of successive prime ministers during the past 30 years, dreamed up these complex graphic games, these pseudo-messages from aliens, in order to pull the wool over everyone's eyes? Have certain British secret services really tried, with success, to manipulate public opinion and the media, and are they continuing to do so today? Have they managed to convince people that these immense works of programmed computer art are laid out on the ground by fringe groups, and to a lesser extent, that extraterrestrials might be involved?

All the answers stem from two certainties: that the crop circles are laid out from the sky, with the aid of high frequency wave technology; and that only the official territorial authorities could "cover" such experiments.

Voyage to the Heart of the Military Bases

We returned to Great Britain, this time as well-informed visitors. We wanted to verify the military character of the region, and to observe the traces left by crop circles. But an article consulted on the Internet, before our departure, had tempered our expectations about this last point. It was titled

"Persistence of an Effect at Crop Circle Sites."[1]

It's said that after the harvest, the field retains the imprint of a crop circle. This claim is quickly contradicted by an on-the-spot check. A friend made a journey in winter 2001 to confirm the presence of these traces in the snow, six months after the harvests. The flanks of Milk Hill, where the most imposing crop circle of the summer of 2001 appeared, were inspected, but no trace was found. Whereas a study by Dr. Levengood established that this formation presented anomalies, and that, consequently, it was authentic. But no, there was nothing to report, either on the snow or on naked ground. Another false rumor.

Our "HQ" was a bed-and-breakfast at West Overton, a tiny and peaceful hamlet located between Marlborough and Avebury. Our host's home was typically English, a charming little cottage where the kindness of the lady of the house was equaled only by her splendid breakfasts. Of course, we questioned her about crop circles. Although she had no idea of their origins, she told us that two patterns had appeared in the field opposite her dwelling one rainy night during the previous summer, something we could easily confirm. Less than 1,000 feet away the traces were still spread on the ground, and more than three months after the end of the harvest season, they were still largely visible.

[1] See http://site.voila.fr/cropcircle.critique/index.jhtml.

We decided to travel, in the space of four days, the most "classic" tourist itinerary. The circuit included the megalithic sites of Silbury/Avebury and Stonehenge, as well as the numerous famous "White Horses" present in the region, which were in fact immense representations of equine figures on the flanks of hills, produced by scratching away the soil to expose the subjacent layer of chalk.

The author examines wheat inside a crop circle
that appeared near Silbury Hill

The figures created in the wheat during the summer season had returned to the state of mere abandoned traces, but these were still vast, and most of them clearly discernable despite the months that had passed since their execution. Several rapid incursions into the harvested (and now muddy) fields permitted us to check on these markings up close and to observe the strange configuration of the flattened wheat.

We also decided to check and observe for ourselves whether the central region of Wiltshire was, in fact, full of British military bases.

Upon exiting from the billiards room of the Barge Inn at Alton Priors,[1] we headed off for Salisbury Plain under a driving rain in order to reach the megalithic site of Stonehenge by way of the village of Pewsey (highway A345).

After the almost deserted small town of Upavon, the highway is bordered, on both sides, by wheat fields adorned at regular intervals with red and yellow warning signs.
These signs read:

> **Danger. Ministry of Defence Range**
> *Do not proceed beyond this point when flags*
> *or lamps are displayed.*

From Upavon (home, among other things, of the Trenchard Line military camp) we drove towards Everleigh to rejoin the A338 highway and make our way down to North Tidworth (where one finds the Tidworth military camp). Other road signs constantly reminded us that we were right in the middle of a perimeter turned over to the

---

[1] *The owner of the Barge Inn, located at Alton Priors (right in the middle of the perimeter of the strongest concentration of crop formations) had transformed a small room of the restaurant into an "agriglyph museum."*

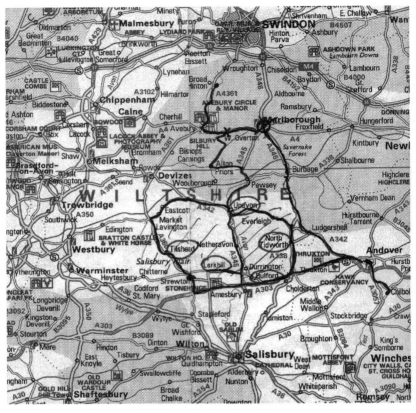

The Investigators' "Expedition"—The map shows areas
that belong to the British army.

exclusive use of the British army. We then went on to
Bulford (and Bulford camp) on the A303, before finally
reaching Stonehenge but not until we had gone astray
several times around Larkhill, within the boundaries of the
military zone known as the Bustard site, after somehow

overlooking a highly visible red sign:

> **Road Closure beyond Bustard Hotel**
> *The roads between Greenlands camp and Westdown camp*
> *are closed to civilian and unauthorized military traffic.*

This little expedition allowed us to become aware of the extent to which this part of Wiltshire was militarized (Michael Glickman told us that it was one of the largest military testing grounds in Europe). After a while, we lost count of the nonstop military maneuvers or the tanks present in the places we traveled through, as they were so numerous. We almost came to believe we were in a war zone.

Might one try to establish a cause-and-effect link between the presence of this giant military base (whose activities are not all public knowledge) and the appearance of crop figures?

Shadow Weapons

Two reports, already cited, seem to pick up on the idea of the military's implication in the agriglyph phenomenon.

During the summer of 1981, when the phenomenon was still just getting underway, two circles of 50 ft. in diameter appeared in a field near Litchfield, at Seven Barrows.[1] During the course of their investigation of this appearance, Pat Delgado and Colin Andrews were hailed by a young local farmer named Tim Martin. The latter thought that the circles could have been made by army helicopters, which he

---

[1] *Mentioned in Chapter One.*

said often flew over the fields. The young man added, "I've heard about similar circles appearing near military zones at Warminster, on Salisbury Plain, as well as Wantage in Oxfordshire."[1]

Again at Litchfield, but the following year, two circles were made, following the usual protocol. They measured, respectively, 30 and 40 ft. in diameter. One curious detail caught the investigators' attention: in addition to the two circles, a semi-circular area had been created just to the north. And this zone presented an important anomaly: the wheat was flattened across a third of the total surface, but the rest of the circle faded out on the adjacent grassy surface.[2] It's hard to believe that circlemakers on the ground would have made such a mistake. In contrast, a bad GPS positioning, or a programming glitch on the part of a military balloon still being tested, would explain this truncated circle.

In an article dated September 12, 1987 in the French magazine *Air & Cosmos,* journalist Yves Brocard gave readers a preview of a very strange experiment that was to take place in Canada, involving the transmission of energy through a microwave beam. The project, baptized SHARP (Stationary High Altitude Relay Platform), would put into operation a remote controlled airplane whose energy was to

---

[1] Circular Evidence, *op cit., p. 19.*
[2] *Ibid, p. 23.*

be supplied by a beam of high frequency microwaves, emitted by powerful generators. Receivers underneath the plane would absorb this energy and convert it into a continuous electrical current that would feed the aircraft's propeller. The plane was only a scale model flying at an altitude of 500 ft. in a "figure eight" in order to remain within the emitted beams. But, according to *Air & Cosmos*, the system's future was promising. An airplane equipped in this fashion, at an altitude of 12 mi., could serve as a "communications relay or surveillance platform." The conjectures of Jean-Paul Piton suddenly began to take on a concrete form.

Doubtless such systems existed even prior to this public announcement by the Canadian Ministry of Communications.

Microwave laser technology is not new, even if the media seems to have just discovered it. It was, in fact, being developed during the 1950s. Under the cover of military secrecy, such a project could proceed completely undetected.

On this point, another article in *Air & Cosmos*, that appeared in issue number 1842, dated May 10, 2002, states:

> *RF (Radio Frequency) and HPM (High-Powered Microwave) weapon systems, better known under the generic terms of electromagnetic or ultrahigh frequency weapons, are indeed likely to be incorporated into the*

panoply of offensive military equipment more quickly than experts had foreseen. These are weapons emitting electromagnetic pulses (of non-nuclear origin), sufficiently energetic to disturb or even destroy the electronics of enemy weapon systems: calculators, self-directed systems, electronic flight controls, etc."

Thus, a ground generator delivering several kilowatts in a few micro- or nanoseconds can send a beam to a reflector system at high altitude that will focus and reflect it back at a ground target.

The analysis of the texture inside a crop circle (the alignment of tufts of the same width arranged as if they had passed through a comb with teeth spaced every few feet) indeed reinforces the idea that low level radiation had passed through the figure causing, through heat, all of the modifications observed in the ears of wheat. As a mobile platform at high altitude moves very slowly compared to the pulse, the ground impact inevitably takes the form of a circle (or several circles), a diffracted image that corresponds with the width of the focused beam (like the point of a pen, in a sense). The energy produced by lasers today is largely sufficient to alter the wheat exactly as one observes on the ground.

HAARP: A Disturbing Project

In the experiments carried out that involve clandestine

research and development of directed beam weaponry, the goal is clear: to be able to damage or destroy a target at any point on the globe. That is precisely what is powerfully evoked by a technology whose existence has been widely reported by the press and about which a book by French author Marc Fiterman, *Les Armes de l'Ombre [Shadow Weapons]* devotes a chapter:[1] HAARP (Highfrequency Active Auroral Research Project). The program made the news two years ago, when some blamed it for the terrible snowstorm of Christmas 1999.

It would be tedious to go into the highly technical details of HAARP. But to sum up, it's a project costing $30 million, under development near Gokona, Alaska, about 200 mi. from Anchorage. Presented by the American military as "merely scientific research on the ionosphere,"[2] it is nevertheless funded by the Department of Defense, the U.S. Air Force, and the U.S. Navy.

The area taken up by the infrastructure necessary for this "mere" scientific study is an immense, flat, deforested plot of land, covered by 48 antennas about 65 ft. tall, each of which is linked to a megawatt power emitter. Eventually, 360 such antennas will occupy the landscape.

In fact, HAARP is the smokescreen for a weapon, henceforth an open secret, based on the most advanced

---

[1] *Editions Carnot, 2001. English translation forthcoming from Carnot USA Books.*
[2] *A layer of high energetic density situated above the stratosphere, or 30 miles over ground level, constituted by ionized particles, both ions and electrons, that protect us from harmful solar radiation.*

technology, possibly the most terrifying in nature that the military will ever succeed in making operational. Magda Aelvoet, a member of the European Parliament and a former leading figure in the Green Party group, tried in vain to bring it to public attention.[1] A good number of armament experts today agree that it entails the creation of an immense "protective shield" inhibiting the navigation systems of missiles or other weapons at any point on Earth. The device

evokes our English crop circle tests; it generates a beam of radio waves in the direction of the ionosphere that then behaves like a giant mirror of ionized gas, against which ground-generated microwave beams can be bounced.

HAARP will be capable of interfering with navigation and/or communications

A laser cannon with its support rig.

systems, destroying or controlling enemy missiles, increasing the internal temperature and altering the cerebral functions of human beings by electromagnetic radiation, and modifying meteorological conditions in a given region by affecting the circulation of winds in the upper atmosphere. And no doubt other "calamities" that we hesitate to even imagine.

Some even believe that the artificial mirror thus created

---

[1] *See the Official* Journal of the European Communities, Agenda for January 28, 1999. *Euro MP Aelvoet has resigned from her seat since this date.*

upon the ionosphere could deflect the emission of a high frequency beam fired from Alaska so that it returns to the English countryside in the form of designs.[1] This scenario seems highly improbable; the microwave beam would have difficulty conserving its coherence over such a distance. And by rebounding off the ionosphere at an altitude of 48 km. it would arrive at an extremely low angle in the English fields, incapable of sculpting the characteristic sharp edges of the agriglyphs. And lastly, the curvature of the Earth would not allow the beam to reach England through a single rebound.

Are the British conducting the development of this "secret weapon" on their own, or are they collaborating in some vast American program that should alarm the entire world?

Those who see an Anglo-American "plot" point to the old "Star Wars" project, nicknamed for the American SDI (Strategic Defense Initiative). In the early 1980s, the SDI promoted by the Reagan presidency aimed at setting up a defense in space against Soviet missiles, in the form of directed beam weapons, which involved equipping small satellites placed in orbit around the Earth. The GBL [Ground Based Laser] project developed, for example, the concept of a ground cannon whose laser, deflected by an array of satellites equipped with reflective mirrors, would have intercepted enemy missiles during their boost phase in order to destroy them.

---

[1] *A hypothesis evoked by a well-known French researcher, through an exchange of private e-mails (thus, we respect his anonymity).*

"Officially," this program was put on hold at the start of the 1990s because of its exorbitant cost, enormous technical constraints, and the collapse of the Soviet bloc.

That does not necessarily mean that the technology developed in the previous period was abandoned.

The May 10, 2002 issue of *Air & Cosmos* affirmed this:

Several countries possess electromagnetic or ultrahigh frequency weapons. Although none have officially acknowledged their possession of "E" bombs,[1] several do admit that they dispose of recurrent ultrahigh frequency weapon systems. The first to acknowledge this was the United States, followed by Sweden, which declared that it had systems capable of stopping vehicles at a distance, and finally Australia, announcing in October 2000 through the intermediary of the Electronic Warfare Division of the DSTO (Defence Science and Technology Division) that it was working on radio frequency weapons.

One could add to this list, without risk of being discredited, the ally of the United States, Israel, whose development and testing of directed beam weapons are widely known (including its involvement with MIRACL [Mid-Infrared Advanced Chemical Laser] an American project tested several years ago at the White Sands Missile Range in New Mexico).

---

[1] *Author's note: electromagnetic bombs.*

As for France, *Air & Cosmos* writes, it

acknowledges that it has conducted for the last decade a 'black program' on ultrahigh frequency weapons. According to experts at the Ministry of Defense, French priorities include, firstly, consumable systems of the 'E' bomb or electromagnetic bomb type [...] based on 'flux compressor generators,' or high voltage generators coupled with high-powered pulses [...] For airborne applications, three types of vectors are envisaged, both on combat drones, or UCAV [Uninhabited Combat Air Vehicles], and in the shorter term, on manned aircraft. 'We are today already able to equip a four meter (13 ft.) long pod with a recurrent HPM (High-Powered Microwave) of several gigawatts in power,' Air & Cosmos was told by experts within Thalès Communication, which is working on ultrahigh frequency weapons.[1]

A Death Ray in a Balloon

Among those who suspect that the United States is implicated in the British tests is a French computer engineer, Emmanuel Delhinger, author of a book still in search of a publisher, but already available online, *Ovnis: L'Armée Démasquée [UFOs: The Army Unmasked].*[2]

---

[1] Air & Cosmos, *n° 1842, May 10, 2002.*
[2] www.ovnis.atfreeweb.com.

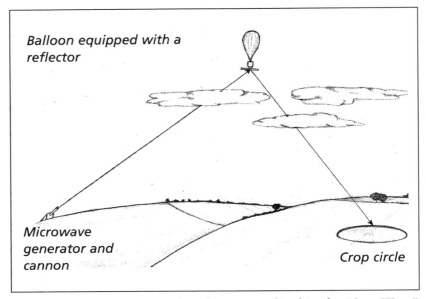

Balloon equipped with a reflector

Microwave generator and cannon

Crop circle

Hypothesis to compare with techniques utilized in the "Star Wars" and HAARP projects: an energy generator based "somewhere" sends microwaves to a high-altitude "relay aircraft" equipped with a reflector, which will send the beam back to the ground in order to flatten the plants and create the figure.

For Delhinger, the Americans possess ultrahigh frequency systems mounted on aircraft, and more particularly, aboard balloons or dirigibles. He thus concurs with the reasoning that permitted "Jean-Paul Piton" to suspect the use of aerostats.

Balloons are used because of their economic advantages (very low cost), their great reliability, and the flexibility of their deployment and launch (they can take off from anywhere, with the help of a mobile crane). Delhinger notes

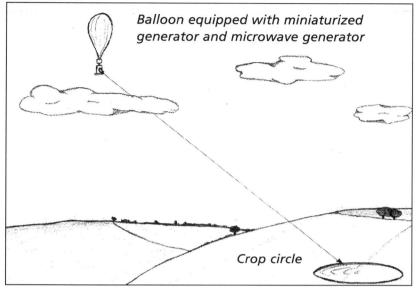

Balloon equipped with miniaturized generator and microwave generator

Crop circle

A hypothesis that is much more probable today according to what we know of advances taking place in the field of miniaturization. The balloon, in this configuration, flies around at a height of a few thousand feet, or even several miles in altitude (for operational reasons on the one hand, and to avoid zones frequented by civilian aircraft on the other). It sends a microwave beam in order to flatten the plants and create a figure on the ground.

their extreme silence in flight, as well as the absence of vibrations, essential for the HPM onboard.

In addition, balloons are capable of attaining very high altitudes, a guarantee of their invisibility from the ground. Aerostats equipped with a microwave laser cannon would therefore be the ideal suspects behind the discreet, quiet elaboration of crop circles.

And, according to the computer engineer, the Americans are (yet again) at the cutting edge in this domain. The HABE (High Altitude Balloon Experiment) research program, under the supervision of the Ballistic Missile Defense Organization, was developed by the U.S. Air Force Research Laboratory's Space Vehicles section at the Kirtland base in New Mexico.

Dirigibles of War

HABE carried out tests of detection, pursuit, and destruction of targets on the ground, through the utilization of microwave cannons attached to stratospheric balloons. These balloons, whose movements were tracked by GPS, rose to altitudes of up to 20 mi. and remained in flight for days and sometimes weeks.

Thus "incognito," such balloons, which are mostly used for scientific purposes, could fly over regions (drifting parallel to the equator) without being held accountable by countries that had signed international accords. That would be convenient, let's say, in order to go to England without having to inform the authorities. For Emmanuel Dehlinger, "a stratospheric balloon normally goes round the world in less than 15 days and all the more rapidly if it flies at a higher altitude where the distance to cover is obviously shorter. In the Northern Hemisphere, it moves east in summer and west the rest of the year. Its trajectory is easier to foresee in summer when it is regular and only oscillates plus or minus five degrees of altitude. It is therefore quite possible to pass directly over the south of England several times during that period of the year when crop circles appear."[1]

As if echoing these calculations by the author of *Ovnis: L'Armée Démasquée, [UFOs: The Military Unmasked]*, the journalist Serge Brosselin, in *Air & Cosmos*, does not exclude the possibility that "the U.S. might also envisage using dirigibles as platforms to intercept cruise missiles or anti-ship missiles."[2]

Such a balloon could be equipped with a maser canon system (already evoked above by our anonymous informant) and piloted by computer, something that certain crop circles indeed suggest through their geometric forms, which include 3-D images and fractals. There remains the question of displacement. How is it possible for a balloon, as stable as it might be, to constitute the platform from which the "circle shooters" will succeed in creating such perfect designs. Dehlinger responds to this point with still more estimates that should be added to the case file:

A small calculation is nevertheless necessary concerning the generation of a crop circle that should take place in under a minute, according to some

---

[1] *Op cit.*
[2] [UFOs: The Military Unmasked]
[3] Air & Cosmos, *December 6, 2002.*

testimonies gathered. During this lapse of time, our balloon will have traveled a distance of 60 sec. X 70 m/s = 4 km. (2.5 mi.). Since it flies at a height of 30 km. (20 miles), this represents an angular displacement of Atg 4/30 = 8 degrees, that is four degrees to one side and the other of the vertical with respect to the circle, which should not pose a problem. Indeed, compared to the height of a ripe wheat stem (90 cm, or 3 ft.), that implies a maximum imprecision of Tg four degrees X 0.9 cm = 6 cm for the design on the ground."

The Shooting Range

So, on paper at least, here is the probable scenario for testing the "weapon" in a balloon:

We are in Wiltshire on a dark and rainy night. The countryside is deserted. Above the clouds, at low or high altitude (that's the advantage of the flexibility of balloons), a shadow drifts in the greatest silence. This "phantom" is a latest generation dirigible balloon, capable of carrying loads weighing several dozen tons, and thus completely equipped with both an electrical generator and a microwave generator. In order to avoid attention, the aircraft flies with its lights extinguished. An infrared "night vision" system as well as radar imaging give the crew a view of the scene below (in black-and-white) through the clouds, with a resolution of about one cm. (less than half an inch). A radar system keeps watch, just in case.

Once again, the airship is ready to "strike." The target is a wheat field several hundred, or even thousands, of feet below, close to the Stonehenge monument. The cannon fires! The onboard electronics calculate constant corrections and in real time adjusts the angle of firing throughout its entire duration. The gyroscopic system supporting the electromagnetic cannon, for its part, maintains a high degree of stability with respect to the point of impact, despite the balloon's speed of displacement.

On the ground, the wheat undergoes intense, rapid heating. The plants fold over in tufts, one after another, like a gigantic set of toppling dominos. A few seconds later, the crop circle has been formed while the balloon continues its tests, before returning to the hangar at its home base. Quick as a flash, and nobody the wiser.

The aerostat bears no identifiable markings. Is the anonymous weapon in the English skies British or American? It's the last unknown of a mystery that has now largely been cleared up.

Crop Circles

Epilogue

> *A lie gets halfway around the world before*
> *the truth has a chance to get its pants on*[1]

The "hoax of the century," we wrote.

The fact that the majority of the crop figures appear on English soil does not, of course, mean that the British authorities have been acting on their own. We just saw that the hypothesis of an entirely American operation attracts plenty of support. The United States is the world's dominant power, possessing bases throughout the world. They are at the forefront in the field of weaponry.

In the last decade, the crop circles phenomenon has been gradually exported to other countries (even if England still accounts for 80 percent of appearances), principally Canada, Israel, the Netherlands, Germany, and the United States (the agriglyphs of Kennewick, 1993, and Chehalis, 1994). In other words, countries that are rather close allies of Uncle Sam.

The agrarian circles that appeared in Israel (at Bet Zarzir in Jezreel valley, and at Tel Yitzhak, in the suburbs of Kadima, in 1997) provided samples that were analyzed by Talbott and Levengood, of the BLT team. They recently established that the plants, like those in certain English

---

[1] *A quotation from that master of deception in the interests of the British state, Sir Winston Churchill (1874-1965).*

samples, had been subjected to a strong magnetization, which is a good indication in favor of their "authenticity." The German circles are also in full expansion (Burghasunsen, in 1999, Malsburg, Stoenkvitz, Ziernberg, Sinsheim, and Escheberg in 2001). And Germany is crammed with "Yankee" bases.

But in that case, can one seriously envisage that the British were not informed of the "work" being carried out by their most steadfast ally? It is very unlikely. Just as it would be very rash to imagine that the top brass of Her Majesty's armed forces are acting on their own, unbeknownst to the United States.

Why was the south of England chosen for the development of the ultrahigh frequency, rather than one of the numerous American bases situated out in the desert, far from prying eyes? Wouldn't "Area 51" (the "forbidden" American military base in Nevada that is the same size as Switzerland), popularized by the Roswell affair, be better suited to hiding an experiment of this kind (although it does lack wheat fields)?

These objections are sensible ones. Despite everything, several arguments remain that seem to deeply implicate Great Britain in the crop circle phenomenon.

– The south of England continues to be a "spiritual pole."

– The idea of creating an association between crop circles

and megaliths in public opinion would have appealed to more than one "psy-ops" officer working for the secret services.

– The fact that French wheat fields neighboring the megalithic sites of Brittany remain devoid of any pictogram validates the idea that extraterrestrials are not "in on the act" and that a military power is pulling the strings. The Americans and/or British would not, after all, dare play games with cereals "made in France."

On the other hand, the fact that Wiltshire is a "fief" of military camps, and that all of their activities are far from known, is a powerful argument in favor of the hypothesis of weapon testing, conducted entirely or in part by the British authorities. After all, the energy generators that high-altitude balloons would need to create microwaves can be hidden there discreetly.

A British Strategy?

Curiously, Britain does not appear in the list of countries which have taken a technological lead in the development of ultrahigh frequency weapons.

But we know that the contribution of Britain to the "Star Wars" program will lead to authorization of the use of the Fylingdales radar base in the north of England. Two years ago, international public opinion was aroused when

European parliamentary members discovered that Britain had been housing, on its territory, the "big space ears" of the "Echelon" spy program. The British government had, of course, received compensation. What advantages does it expect to derive from placing its sites in future at the disposal of the North American surveillance network directed from NORAD? No doubt it will benefit (if needed) from the protection of American pursuit radar. In that case, the system at work above the English fields could quite possibly be an anti-missile weapon.

Remember that during our first meeting with the engineer who alerted us to the microwaves being used as a "pen" to draw crop circles, this necessarily anonymous scientist refused, in the strict framework of his analysis, to evoke the underlying political and military aspects of this foolish game.

In the course of a second meeting, however, still under the cover of the "Jean-Paul Piton" pseudonym, this representative of a French defense agency talked to us about his hypothesis. According to him, it could not be ruled out that the whole affair was an entirely British strategic defense initiative.

● ● ●

Jean-Paul Piton:

If we are in the presence of an HPM system (High-Powered Microwave) it's not intended to fire salvos from the sky. The set-up capable of sculpting wheat with precision from 20 mi. away could, with all the more reason, reach objects in flight from the ground. I therefore think that it can only be a directed beam weapon that, on the ground, would be capable, through high-powered, recurrent ultrahigh frequency pulses, of disturbing, if not destroying in flight, the electronics of enemy weapon systems: calculators, self-directed systems, flight controls, etc.

In the present case, it would be sufficient to invert the system utilized in the creation of crop circles. The HPM generator is no longer aboard a stabilized platform, but anchored to the ground, eliminating at the same time the difficulties entailed by a generator at high altitude and by the stability of the instrument while in flight.

But the British would still have to master the detection and pursuit in real time of the target, whether a plane, missile, or even a satellite. There, the Americans' experience is no doubt necessary. They are the only ones, for nearly 10 years now, to have attempted the interception of targets at a distance of several hundred miles, with a success rate of nearly 50 percent.

Initially, one needs to detect and identify the target, then not release it until the triggering of destructive fire by missile, chemical laser, or HPM. All these techniques of detection and pursuit call upon the network of detection and telecommunications satellites and the reception stations deployed by the American army across the entire planet. Thus, the placement of this system at the disposal of their British allies seems probable to me. In exchange, the firing system perfected by the British, thanks to the 'CC' operation would no doubt be useful to the American military. Notably the goniometric[1] aiming head.

• • •

So, are the military in the U.K. keeping big secrets? It wouldn't be the first time. During the Second World War, the British succeeded in fooling the German secret services by making them believe the Allied debarkation would take place on the Belgian coast, all the while preparing the Normandy landings. They did so by building cleverly camouflaged fake ports where barges were loaded with trucks and tanks were made out of cardboard!

From that enormous bluff to the crop circles, the spirit remains the same.

---

[1] *Goniometry is a means utilized in navigation (aerial or naval) to take one's bearings. The principle is based on the detection of a signal emission by a beacon. The goniometric system is designed to determine the direction of this beacon.*

The insular character of the British, a theme harped upon by Anglophobes, evokes the terrible aerial bombardments, on London in particular, that were carried out in World War II by the German air force, relayed by the V1 then V2 missiles. The British in general, and their army in particular (which one can readily understand) have continued to be haunted by the memory of these aerial attacks.

And it leads one to think that the protection of their airspace has been enshrined as a national priority. Now deprived of the Australian deserts where they formerly carried out nuclear tests, have they found, through pragmatism, daring, and deception, a way of compensating for this difficulty on their own territory? Whatever the case may be, nothing prevents us from perceiving a logic in the rhythm of these crop circle "tests." Each year, at the end of spring and beginning of summer, the experimenters collect a series of "measurements" in real time through the agriglyph game, which allows them to validate, improve, start over, etc. during the winter.

If this reasoning has any basis in reality, it is probable that the recurrent HPM weapon system is today close to the operational phase. One should then, in the course of coming years, expect the "magical" source of the crop circles to begin to peter out.

The sky artists in uniform have achieved near perfection. They have incidentally generated hundreds of Web sites, reinvigorated the "Little Grays" as an urban myth, enriched photographers, and even a few authors. But through this little game of hide-and-seek they are playing, they are fueling the discourse of hateful cults and risking the lives of innocent bystanders. Despite all the precautions the weapon operators undoubtedly take (the detection of human presence, their choice of sites, pinpointing the target) it can never rule out the possibility that an ultrahigh frequency beam may strike a stray walker in the middle of the night. This person would be killed on the spot, as if he or she found themselves in a giant microwave oven. Some remains of English hedgehogs and other "cooked" animals give some idea of the risks. The magazine *Effervesciences* claims that, "in a crop circle, a dead bird was found whose body had literally exploded, as if it had been cooked alive in a microwave oven. In other formations, dried-up hedgehogs have been found."[1]

The French cereologist already cited, an adept of the mystical explanation of crop circles, told us during her lecture a naive anecdote that should be classified among the cases of animal "cooking." She said that she noticed one day the black feathers of a crow in one of the lines of an

[1] Effervesciences (www.effervesciences.com, *51 route d'Espagne, 31100 Toulouse, France) is a serious scientific review that does not hesitate to explore areas routinely ignored by "orthodox science."*

agriglyph. Persuaded that these feathers were showing her a path [sic], she followed them, only to find the poor crow who had scattered them—she erected a sort of grain tomb for it, burying the body beneath the wheat at the center of the circle. We think rather that this crow was a victim of the British army, and that its feathers, far from "showing a path," instead underline the dangers posed to humans by the weapons being tested. Michael Glickman, the architect and crop circle fan we met in England, told us about the case of wild rabbits that had apparently been struck by microwaves in some Canadian agriglyphs. These little victims found dead on the field of honor also demonstrate the powerful ingenuity of this military disinformation that has managed, thanks to this absurd idea, to disguise an arsenal of death, even letting the most gullible cereologists believe that this terrifying manipulation is a message of cosmic love.

Does the end justify the means? Should we accept that national interests authorize our governments and the armies they control to lie to us and manipulate us?

Crop Circles

Appendices

Messages to Be Read From the Sky

Drawings, engravings, immense scrapings, and messages intended to be read from the sky have existed from the dawn of time. For instance, those in the Pampa plain of Peru, where the Nazca people drew superb geoglyphs, without even being familiar with the wheel. Other examples include the lines 21 mi. long that have been found in the *antiplano* of Bolivia; the 30 ft. wide "highways" that fan out over dozens of miles around Chaco Canyon in the United States and the heart of the Magic Wheel in the Bighorn mountains of Wyoming. Then there is the Wheel of Ensérune (near the town of Béziers), the only geoglyph that exists in France. These silent, incomprehensible testimonies, bequeathed by prodigious ancestors, are associated in our imaginations with the "writing" of giants, gods, and, for some, extraterrestrials.

These are far from the ephemeral images of the crop circles. Yet, these mute figures play on the same register— they try to pass themselves off as messages needing to be deciphered. But according to us, they are nothing but decoys.

With the "hype" surrounding the release of M. Night Shyamalan's film, *Signs,* the loop is complete. It is suggested that the agriglyphs are messages of great intellectual value that could save humanity from decline. From this perspective, all interpretative fantasies are equally valid. The crop circles are gradually turning humans to an alternative "state of consciousness;" they are the result of unknown terrestrial spiritual energies, etc. The scientific controversy has not changed this. On the contrary, in fact, everything seems to happen in a way that indicates that the military experimenters we suspect behind the pictogram are subtly, slowly, and in small doses, using our fears, our myths, and our taste for the unexplained, to enshrine the crop circle as a kind of magical act. In this fashion, the whole crop circle operation may have been conceived with great intelligence by military strategists. Even the distressing agriglyphs at Chilbolton (the aliens and their fake message) which seemed to be clumsy attempts at diversion. These were effective, however, with the ufologists and cults.

Were the inventors of crop circles inspired by primitive forms from human prehistory? One is tempted to believe so looking at the "circles" and round shapes carved in the stone, much smaller than the giant circles drawn in the fields. These cups and rings, veritable basic models for the crop circle programmers, are deeply rooted in the human psyche.

Hermetic symbols constituted by circles, points, and spirals

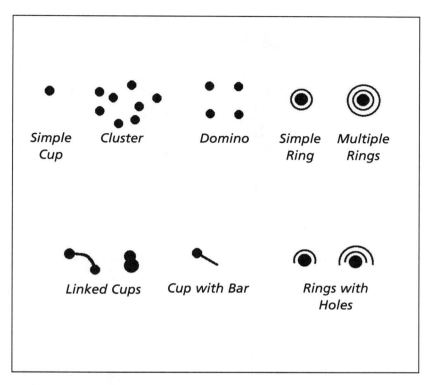

"Cups and Rings," engravings from Northumberland

have been found in the panoply of English pictograms that have appeared in the fields between 1978 and the beginning of the 1990s. Is it an attempt to incite our unconscious to seek the key to deciphering mysteries beyond Earth?

Above, from across the millennia, is the catalogue of the pictograms that perhaps inspired the chief designers of one of the greatest operations in history of state-directed deception.

Another example of similarities between a form of prehistoric symbolic drawing and the silhouette of a real agriglyph.

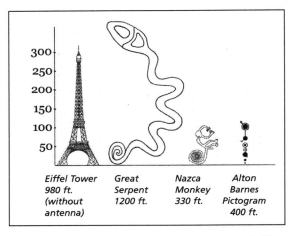

Comparative sizes (in meters) among different geoglyphs and the Eiffel Tower.

The last two drawings are the primitive forms found on rocks and standing stones. Above, the references to crop circles that could have been inspired by them.

Were British Army Engineers ingenious enough to tap into this primitive symbolism?

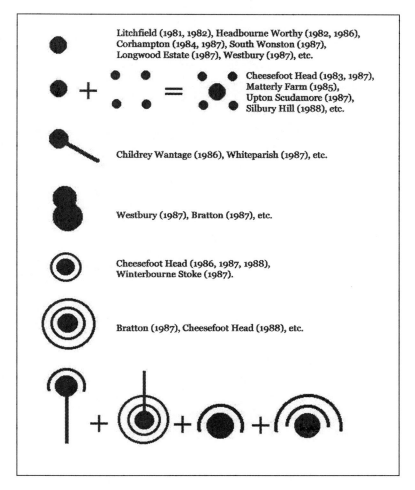

From 1990, the appearance of the pictograms that combine all of the symbols.

Crop Circles

Crop Circle Hunter

Name: Steve Alexander. Age: 43 years. Nationality: British. This professional photographer has little by little devoted most of his iconographic business to agriglyphs. This documentary material is in such demand throughout the world that it allows many professionals to devote themselves to its exploitation.

How long have you been taking photos of the agriglyphs?
I took my first pictures in 1993.

Do you have your own airplane?
Not yet! In fact, I rent a helicopter.

Did you launch into this adventure with an eye to creating a lucrative business out of it?
Oh, not really. After having taken photographs of the crop circles on the ground, out of curiosity and interest I rented my first 'copter in 1994. And from then on, I was approached spontaneously by people who wanted to buy my photographs.

But you are not the only person to offer such pictures? Is competition tough?
Yes, a little. I built my collection of pictures year after year, and I constantly tried to improve their quality. The competition revolves around that aspect. I am a "pro" from beginning to end in my approach. But that's not the case of

a good number of photographers specializing in crop circles.

What kind of camera do you use?
A Nikon FM2 35 mm.

How do you find out about the appearance of agriglyphs?
Generally, it's Mark Fussel, of the Crop Circle Connector Web site *[www.cropcircleconnector.com]* who alerts us to new designs. But more and more, motivated witnesses contact us directly.

Have you ever noticed malfunctioning of your equipment inside an agriglyph?
I once had the misfortune of a new camera battery discharging completely inside an agriglyph at Telegraph Hill in Hampshire. I had set the camera down on the ground to use another. And the battery of that one was dead as well! Once I got home, I saw that the batteries had both returned to their normal charge level.

Who buys your pictures?
Private individuals, most of the time, rather than the media. But I do sell my pictures to them.

Do you know the number of agriglyphs that have appeared since 1978?
Not exactly. But there have been thousands.

Who is making these fantastic designs?
The question of "who" is making them doesn't seem important to me. The agriglyphs have changed peoples' lives. They open our consciousness to other realities, other possibilities. They are archetypical images that inspire and stimulate and interact with us more on an individual than a collective level. They establish a definite link with something that is not from our world, as is suggested also by those strange "balls of lights" in or near the designs.

Crop Circles

BIBLIOGRAPHY

Andrews, Colin and Pat Delgado. *Circular Evidence*, Bloomsbury, 1989.

Beckensall, Stan. *Prehistoric Rock Art in Northumberland*, Tempus Publishing Ltd., 2001.

Devereux, Paul and Ian Thomson. *The Leyhunters Companion*, Thames and Hudson Ltd., 1979.

Haselhoff, Eltjo. *The Deepening Complexity of Crop Circles: Scientific Research and Urban Legends*, Frog Ltd. 2001.

Marciniak, Barbara. *Bringers of the Dawn: Teachings from the Pleiadians*, Bear & Co., 1992.

Meaden, G. Terence. *The Circles Effect and its Mysteries*, Artetech, 1989.

Mitchell, John. *The Flying Saucer Vision: The Holy Grail Restored*, Sidgwick Jackson, 1967.

Picknett, Lynn & Clive Prince, *The Stargate Conspiracy: The Truth About Extraterrestrial Life and the Mysteries of Ancient Egypt*, Berkley, 2001.

Sagan, Carl. *The Cosmic Connection: An Extraterrestrial Perspective*, Anchor Press, 1974.

Story, Ronald D. *The Encyclopedia of UFOs*, Dolphin Books/Doubleday & Co., 1980.

Wilson, Colin. *Alien Dawn: An Investigation into the Contact Experience*, Virgin Publishing, Ltd., 1998.